RCMP Practice!

RCMP Police Aptitude (RPAT) Practice Test Questions

Published by

Complete TEST™ Preparation Inc.

Copyright © 2016 by Complete Test Preparation Inc. ALL RIGHTS RESERVED. No part of this book may be reproduced or transferred in any form or by any means, graphic, electronic, or mechanical, including photocopying, recording, web distribution, taping, or by any information storage retrieval system, without the written permission of the author.

Notice: Complete Test Preparation Inc. makes every reasonable effort to obtain from reliable sources accurate, complete, and timely information about the tests covered in this book. Nevertheless, changes can be made in the tests or the administration of the tests at any time and Complete Test Preparation Inc. makes no representation or warranty, either expressed or implied as to the accuracy, timeliness, or completeness of the information contained in this book. Complete Test Preparation Inc. makes no representations or warranties of any kind, express or implied, about the completeness, accuracy, reliability, suitability or availability with respect to the information contained in this document for any purpose. Any reliance you place on such information is therefore strictly at your own risk.

The author(s) shall not be liable for any loss incurred as a consequence of the use and application, directly or indirectly, of any information presented in this work. Sold with the understanding, the author(s) is not engaged in rendering professional services or advice. If advice or expert assistance is required, the services of a competent professional should be sought.

The company, product and service names used in this publication are for identification purposes only. All trademarks and registered trademarks are the property of their respective owners. Complete Test Preparation Inc. is not affiliated with any educational institution.

Complete Test Preparation Inc. is not affiliated with any RCMP Service, who are not involved in the production of, and do not endorse this publication.

We strongly recommend that students check with exam providers for up-to-date information regarding test content.

ISBN-13: 9781772451382

Version 7.5 February 2019

Published by
Complete Test Preparation Inc.
Victoria BC Canada
Visit us on the web at https://www.test-preparation.ca
Printed in the USA

About Complete Test Preparation Inc.

The Complete Test Preparation Team has been publishing high quality study materials since 2005. Over one million students from all over the world visit our websites every year, and thousands of students, teachers and parents all over the world (over 100 countries) have purchased our teaching materials, curriculum, study guides and practice tests.

Complete Test Preparation is committed to providing students with the best study materials and practice tests available on the market. Members of our team combine years of teaching experience, with experienced writers and editors, all with advanced degrees.

Feedback

We welcome your feedback. Email us at feedback@test-preparation.ca with your comments and suggestions. We carefully review all suggestions and often incorporate reader suggestions into upcoming versions. As a Print on Demand Publisher, we update our products frequently.

 **Find us on Facebook**

www.facebook.com/CompleteTestPreparation

Contents

6   **Getting Started**
        The RCMP Study Plan   8
        Making a Study Schedule   9

14   **Practice Test Questions Set 1**
        Answer Key   44

58   **Practice Test Questions Set 2**
        Answer Key   105

120   **Conclusion**

Getting Started

CONGRATULATIONS! By deciding to take the RCMP Police Aptitude Test, you have taken the first step toward a great future! Of course, there is no point in taking this important examination unless you intend to do your very best to earn the highest grade you possibly can. That means getting yourself organized and discovering the best approaches, methods and strategies to master the material. Yes, that will require real effort and dedication on your part, but if you are willing to focus your energy and devote the study time necessary, before you know it you will be on you way to a brighter future!

We know that taking on a new endeavour can be scary, and it is easy to feel unsure of where to begin. That's where we come in. This study guide is designed to help you improve your test-taking skills, show you a few tricks of the trade

and increase both your competency and confidence.

The RCMP Police Aptitude Test

The RCMP is composed of six sections,

Observation – This section tests your ability to remember details

- **Reading Comprehension**
- **Composition** – This section tests your ability to articulate in writing, complex thoughts in a clear and concise way that is understandable to others. This includes, vocabulary, spelling and English grammar.

- **Professional Judgment**

- **Recognition/Identification** — Here you are shown a face and asked to choose the same person from four pictures, where their appearance has been altered.

- **Logic** — This section tests your ability to analyze situations. Questions include, ordering pieces of information into a logical sequence, reading a map, identifying patterns in data, and solving problems

- **Simple Word Problems** (Basic Math)

While we seek to make our guide as comprehensive as possible, note that like all exams, the RCMP Exam might be adjusted at some future point. New material might be added, or content that is no longer relevant or applicable might be removed. It is always a good idea to give the materials you receive when you register to take the RCMP test a careful review.

The RCMP Study Plan

Now that you have made the decision to take the RCMP test, it is time to get started. Before you do another thing, you will need to figure out a plan of attack. The very best study tip is to start early! The longer the time period you devote to regular study practice, the more likely you will be to retain the material and be able to access it quickly. If you thought that 1x20 is the same as 2x10, guess what? It really is not, when it comes to study time. Reviewing material for just an hour per day over the course of 20 days is far better than studying for two hours a day for only 10 days. The more often you revisit a particular piece of information, the better you will know it. Not only will your grasp and understanding be better, but your ability to reach into your brain and quickly and efficiently pull out the tidbit you need, will be greatly enhanced as well.

The great Chinese scholar and philosopher Confucius believed that true knowledge could be defined as knowing both what you know and what you do not know. The first step in preparing for the RCMP is to assess your strengths and weaknesses. You may already have an idea of what you know and what you do not know, but evaluating yourself using our Self- Assessment modules for each of the test content areas may surprise you.

Making a Study Schedule

To make your study time the most productive, you will need to develop a study plan. The purpose of the plan is to organize all the bits of pieces of information in such a way that you will not feel overwhelmed. Rome was not built in a day, and learning everything you will need to know to pass the RCMP is going to take time, too. Arranging the material you need to learn into manageable chunks is the best way to go. Each study session should make you feel as though you have succeeded in accomplishing your goal, and your goal is simply to learn what you planned to learn during that particular session. Try to organize the content in such a way that each study session builds on previous ones. That way, you will retain the information, be better able to access it, and review the previous bits and pieces at the same time.

Self-assessment

The Best Study Tip! The very best study tip is to start early! The longer you study regularly, the more you will retain and 'learn' the material. Studying for 1 hour per day for 20 days is far better than studying for 2 hours for 10 days.

What don't you know?

The first step is to assess your strengths and weaknesses. You may already have an idea of where your weaknesses are, or you can take our Self-assessment modules for each of the content areas.

Exam Component	Rate 1 to 5
Reading Comprehension	
Composition	
Vocabulary	
Spelling	
English Grammar	
Professional Judgment	
Recognition/Identification	
Logic	
Ordering information	
Identifying sequences	
Solving Problems	
Basic Math	
Percent	
Decimals	
Word Problems	

Making a Study Schedule

The key to making a study plan is to divide the material you need to learn into manageable sized pieces and learn it, while at the same time reviewing the material that you already know.
Using the table above, any scores of 3 or below, you need to

spend time learning, reviewing and practicing this subject area. A score of 4 means you need to review the material, but you don't have to spend time re-learning. A score of 5 and you are OK with just an occasional review before the exam.
A score of 0 or 1 means you really need to work on this should allocate the most time and the highest priority.
Some students prefer a 5-day plan and others a 10-day plan. It also depends on how much time you have until the exam.

Here is an example of a 5-day plan based on an example from the table above:

Reading Comprehension: 1- Study 1 hour everyday – review on last day
Vocabulary: 3 - Study 1 hour for 3 days then ½ hour a day, then review
Word Problems: 4 - Review every second day
Professional Judgment: 5 - Review for ½ hour every other day
Logic: 5 - Review for ½ hour every other day

Using this example, logic and professional judgment are good, and only need occasional review. Vocabulary is good and needs 'some' review. Reading Comprehension is very weak and need most of your time.   Based on this, here is a sample study plan:

Day	Subject	Time
Monday		
Study	Reading Comprehension	1 hour
Study	Word Problems	1 hour
½ hour break		
Study	Vocabulary	1 hour
Review	Reading Comp.	½ hour
Tuesday		
Study	Reading Comprehension	1 hour
Study	Word Problems	½ hour
½ hour break		
Study	Vocabulary	½ hour
Review	Professional Judgment	½ hour
Review	Logic	½ hour
Wednesday		
Study	Reading Comprehension	1 hour
Study	Word Problems	½ hour
½ hour break		
Study	Vocabulary	½ hour
Review	Reading Comp.	½ hour
Thursday		
Study	Reading Comprehension	½ hour
Study	Word Problems	½ hour
Review	Vocabulary	½ hour
½ hour break		
Review	Logic	½ hour
Review	Professional Judgment	½ hour
Friday		
Review	Reading Comprehension	½ hour
Review	Word Problems	½ hour
Review	Vocabulary	½ hour
½ hour break		
Review	Professional Judgment	½ hour
Review	Logic	½ hour

Using this example, adapt the study plan to your own schedule. This schedule assumes 2 ½ - 3 hours available to study everyday for a 5 day period.

First, write out what you need to study and how much. Next figure out how many days before the test. Note, do NOT study on the last day before the test. On the last day before the test, you won't learn anything and will probably only confuse yourself.

Make a table with the days before the test and the number of hours you have available to study each day. We suggest working with 1 hour and ½ hour time slots.

Start filling in the blanks, with the subjects you need to study the most getting the most time and the most regular time slots (i.e. everyday) and the subjects that you know getting the least time (e.g. ½ hour every other day, or every 3rd day).

Tips for making a schedule

Once you make a schedule, stick with it! Make your study sessions reasonable. If you make a study schedule and don't stick with it, you set yourself up for failure. Instead, schedule study sessions that are a bit shorter and set yourself up for success! Make sure your study sessions are do-able. Studying is hard work, but after you pass, you can party and take a break!

Schedule breaks. Breaks are just as important as study time. Work out a rotation of studying and breaks that works for you.

Build up study time. If you find it hard to sit still and study for 1 hour straight through, build up to it. Start with 20 minutes, and then take a break. Once you get used to 20-minute study sessions, increase the time to 30 minutes. Gradually work you way up to 1 hour.

40 minutes to 1 hour is optimal. Studying for longer than this is tiring and not productive. Studying for shorter isn't long enough to be productive.

Studying Math. Studying Math is different from studying other subjects because you use a different part of your brain. The best way to study math is to practice everyday. This will train your mind to think in a mathematical way. If you miss a day or days, the mathematical mind-set is gone, and you have to start all over again to build it up.

Study and practice math everyday for at least 5 days before the exam.

Practice Test Questions
Set 1

THE QUESTIONS BELOW ARE NOT THE SAME AS YOU WILL FIND ON THE RCMP ENTRANCE TEST- THAT WOULD BE TOO EASY! And nobody knows what the questions will be and they change all the time. Below are general questions that cover the same subject areas as the RCMP Entrance Test. So, while the format and exact wording of the questions may differ slightly, and change from year to year, if you can answer the questions below, you will have no problem with the RCMP Entrance Test.

For the best results, take these practice test questions as if it were the real exam. Set aside time when you will not be disturbed, and a location that is quiet and free of distractions. Read the instructions carefully, read each question carefully, and answer to the best of your ability.

Use the bubble answer sheets provided. When you have completed the practice questions, check your answer against the Answer Key and read the explanation provided.

Do not attempt more than one set of practice test questions in one day. After completing the first practice test, wait two or three days before attempting the second set of questions.

Reading Comprehension - 20 Questions

Observation – 7 Questions

Professional Judgment: 10 Questions

Recognition/Identification – 3 Questions

Composition – 20 questions

Math - 20 questions

Logic – 20 questions

Reading Comprehension

	A	B	C	D
1	○	○	○	○
2	○	○	○	○
3	○	○	○	○
4	○	○	○	○
5	○	○	○	○
6	○	○	○	○
7	○	○	○	○
8	○	○	○	○
9	○	○	○	○
10	○	○	○	○
11	○	○	○	○
12	○	○	○	○
13	○	○	○	○
14	○	○	○	○
15	○	○	○	○
16	○	○	○	○
17	○	○	○	○
18	○	○	○	○
19	○	○	○	○
20	○	○	○	○

Judgment, Recognition and Observation

	A	B	C	D
1	○	○	○	○
2	○	○	○	○
3	○	○	○	○
4	○	○	○	○
5	○	○	○	○
6	○	○	○	○
7	○	○	○	○
8	○	○	○	○
9	○	○	○	○
10	○	○	○	○
11	○	○	○	○
12	○	○	○	○
13	○	○	○	○
14	○	○	○	○
15	○	○	○	○
16	○	○	○	○
17	○	○	○	○
18	○	○	○	○
19	○	○	○	○
20	○	○	○	○

Composition

```
    A B C D
 1  ○ ○ ○ ○
 2  ○ ○ ○ ○
 3  ○ ○ ○ ○
 4  ○ ○ ○ ○
 5  ○ ○ ○ ○
 6  ○ ○ ○ ○
 7  ○ ○ ○ ○
 8  ○ ○ ○ ○
 9  ○ ○ ○ ○
10  ○ ○ ○ ○
11  ○ ○ ○ ○
12  ○ ○ ○ ○
13  ○ ○ ○ ○
14  ○ ○ ○ ○
15  ○ ○ ○ ○
16  ○ ○ ○ ○
17  ○ ○ ○ ○
18  ○ ○ ○ ○
19  ○ ○ ○ ○
20  ○ ○ ○ ○
```

Math

	A	B	C	D
1	○	○	○	○
2	○	○	○	○
3	○	○	○	○
4	○	○	○	○
5	○	○	○	○
6	○	○	○	○
7	○	○	○	○
8	○	○	○	○
9	○	○	○	○
10	○	○	○	○
11	○	○	○	○
12	○	○	○	○
13	○	○	○	○
14	○	○	○	○
15	○	○	○	○
16	○	○	○	○
17	○	○	○	○
18	○	○	○	○
19	○	○	○	○
20	○	○	○	○

Logic

	A	B	C	D
1	○	○	○	○
2	○	○	○	○
3	○	○	○	○
4	○	○	○	○
5	○	○	○	○
6	○	○	○	○
7	○	○	○	○
8	○	○	○	○
9	○	○	○	○
10	○	○	○	○
11	○	○	○	○
12	○	○	○	○
13	○	○	○	○
14	○	○	○	○
15	○	○	○	○
16	○	○	○	○
17	○	○	○	○
18	○	○	○	○
19	○	○	○	○
20	○	○	○	○

Part I - Reading Comprehension

Questions 1 – 4 refer to the following passage.

Passage 1 - The Life of Helen Keller

Many people have heard of Helen Keller. She is famous because she was unable to see or hear, but learned to speak and read and went onto attend college and earn a degree. Her life is a very interesting story, one that she developed into an autobiography, which was then adapted into both a stage play and a movie. How did Helen Keller overcome her disabilities to become a famous woman? Read onto find out. Helen Keller was not born blind and deaf. When she was a small baby, she had a very high fever for several days. As a result of her sudden illness, baby Helen lost her eyesight and her hearing. Because she was so young when she went deaf and blind, Helen Keller never had any recollection of being able to see or hear. Since she could not hear, she could not learn to talk. Since she could not see, it was difficult for her to move around. For the first six years of her life, her world was very still and dark.

Imagine what Helen's childhood was like. She could not hear her mother's voice. She could not see the beauty of her parent's farm. She could not recognize who was giving her a hug, or a bath or even where her bedroom was each night. More sad, she could not communicate with her parents in any way. She could not express her feelings or tell them the things she wanted. It must have been a very sad childhood.

When Helen was six years old, her parents hired her a teacher named Anne Sullivan. Anne was a young woman who was almost blind. However, she could hear and she could read Braille, so she was a perfect teacher for young Helen. At first, Anne had a very hard time teaching Helen anything. She described her first impression of Helen as a "wild thing, not a child." Helen did not like Anne at first either. She bit and hit Anne when Anne tried to teach her. However, the two of them eventually came to have a great deal of love and respect.

Anne taught Helen to hear by putting her hands on people's throats. She could feel the sounds that people made. In time, Helen learned to feel what people said. Next, Anne taught Helen to read Braille, which is a way that books are written for the blind. Finally, Anne taught Helen to talk. Although Helen did learn to talk, it was hard for anyone but Anne to understand her.

As Helen grew older, more and more people were amazed by her story. She went to college and wrote books about her life. She gave talks to the public, with Anne at her side, translating her words. Today, both Anne Sullivan and Helen Keller are famous women who are respected for their lives' work.

1. Helen Keller could not see and hear and so, what was her biggest problem in childhood?

    a. Inability to communicate
    b. Inability to walk
    c. Inability to play
    d. Inability to eat

2. Helen learned to hear by feeling the vibrations people made when they spoke. What were these vibrations were felt through?

    a. Mouth
    b. Throat
    c. Ears
    d. Lips

3. From the passage, we can infer that Anne Sullivan was a patient teacher. We can infer this because

    a. Helen hit and bit her and Anne still remained her teacher.

    b. Anne taught Helen to read only.

    c. Anne was hard of hearing too.

    d. Anne wanted to be a teacher.

4. Helen Keller learned to speak but Anne translated her words when she spoke in public. The reason Helen needed a translator was because

    a. Helen spoke another language.

    b. Helen's words were hard for people to understand.

    c. Helen spoke very quietly.

    d. Helen did not speak but only used sign language.

Questions 5 – 6 refer to the following passage.

Passage 2 - Ways Characters Communicate in Theatre

Playwrights give their characters voices in a way that gives depth and added meaning to what happens on stage during their play. There are different types of speech in scripts that allow characters to talk with themselves, with other characters, and even with the audience.

It is very unique to theatre that characters may talk "to themselves." When characters do this, the speech they give is called a soliloquy. Soliloquies are usually poetic, introspective, moving, and can tell audience members about the feelings, motivations, or suspicions of an individual character without that character having to reveal them to other characters on stage. "To be or not to be" is a famous soliloquy given by Hamlet as he considers difficult but important themes, such as life and death.

The most common type of communication in plays is when one character is speaking to another or a group of other characters. This is generally called dialogue, but can also be called monologue if one character speaks without being interrupted for a long time. It is not necessarily the most important type of communication, but it is the most common because the plot of the play cannot really progress without it.

Lastly, and most unique to theatre (although it has been used somewhat in film) is when a character speaks directly to the audience. This is called an aside, and scripts usually specifically direct actors to do this. Asides are usually comical, an inside joke between the character and the audience, and very short. The actor will usually face the audience when delivering them, even if it's for a moment, so the audience can recognize this move as an aside.

All three of these types of communication are important to the art of theatre, and have been perfected by famous playwrights like Shakespeare. Understanding these types of communication can help an audience member grasp what is artful about the script and action of a play.

5. According to the passage, characters in plays communicate to

    a. move the plot forward

    b. show the private thoughts and feelings of one character

    c. make the audience laugh

    d. add beauty and artistry to the play

6. The author uses parentheses to punctuate "although it has been used somewhat in film,"

    a. to show that films are less important

    b. instead of using commas so that the sentence is not interrupted

    c. because parenthesis help separate details that are not as important

    d. to show that films are not as artistic

Questions 7 – 9 refer to the following passage.

Passage 3 - Low Blood Sugar

As the name suggest, low blood sugar is low sugar levels in the bloodstream. This can occur when you have not eaten properly and undertake strenuous activity, or, when you are very hungry. When Low blood sugar occurs regularly and is ongoing, it is a medical condition called hypoglycemia. This condition can occur in diabetics and in healthy adults.

Causes of low blood sugar can include excessive alcohol consumption, metabolic problems, stomach surgery, pancreas, liver or kidneys problems, as well as a side-effect of some medications.

Symptoms

There are different symptoms depending on the severity of the case.

Mild hypoglycemia can lead to feelings of nausea and hunger. The patient may also feel nervous, jittery and have fast heart beats. Sweaty skin, clammy and cold skin are likely symptoms.

Moderate hypoglycemia can result in a short temper, confusion, nervousness, fear and blurring of vision. The patient may feel weak and unsteady.

Severe cases of hypoglycemia can lead to seizures, coma, fainting spells, nightmares, headaches, excessive sweats and severe tiredness.

Diagnosis of low blood sugar

A doctor can diagnosis this medical condition by asking the patient questions and testing blood and urine samples. Home testing kits are available for patients to monitor blood sugar levels. It is important to see a qualified doctor though. The doctor can administer tests to ensure that will safely rule out other medical conditions that could affect blood sugar levels.

Treatment

Quick treatments include drinking or eating foods and drinks with high sugar contents. Good examples include soda, fruit juice, hard candy and raisins. Glucose energy tablets can also help. Doctors may also recommend medications and well as changes in diet and exercise routine to treat chronic low blood sugar.

7. Based on the article, which of the following is true?

a. Low blood sugar can happen to anyone.

b. Low blood sugar only happens to diabetics.

c. Low blood sugar can occur even.

d. None of the statements are true.

8. Which of the following are the author's opinion?

a. Quick treatments include drinking or eating foods and drinks with high sugar contents.

b. None of the statements are opinions.

c. This condition can occur in diabetics and also in healthy adults.

d. There are different symptoms depending on the severity of the case

9. Which of the following is not a detail?

a. A doctor can diagnosis this medical condition by asking the patient questions and testing.

b. A doctor will test blood and urine samples.

c. Glucose energy tablets can also help.

d. Home test kits monitor blood sugar levels.

d. None of the above.

Questions 10 – 13 refer to the following passage.

How To Get A Good Nights Sleep

Sleep is just as essential for healthy living as water, air and food. Sleep allows the body to rest and replenish depleted energy levels. Sometimes we may for various reasons experience difficulty sleeping which has a serious effect on our health. Those who have prolonged sleeping problems are facing a serious medical condition and should see a qualified doctor when possible for help. Here is simple guide that can help you sleep better at night.

Try to create a natural pattern of waking up and sleeping around the same time everyday. This means avoiding going to bed too early and oversleeping past your usual wake up time. Going to bed and getting up at radically different times everyday confuses your body clock. Try to establish a natural rhythm as much as you can.

Exercises and a bit of physical activity can help you sleep better at night. If you are having problem sleeping, try to be as active as you can during the day. If you are tired from physical activity, falling asleep is a natural and easy process for your body. If you remain inactive during the day, you will find it harder to sleep properly at night. Try walking, jogging, swimming or simple stretches as you get close to your bed time.

Afternoon naps are great to refresh you during the day, but they may also keep you awake at night. If you feel sleepy during the day, get up, take a walk and get busy to keep from sleeping. Stretching is a good way to increase blood flow to the brain and keep you alert so that you don't sleep during the day. This will help you sleep better night.

> A warm bath or a glass of milk in the evening can help your body relax and prepare for sleep. A cold bath will wake you up and keep you up for several hours. Also avoid eating too late before bed.

10. How would you describe this sentence?

   a. A recommendation
   b. An opinion
   c. A fact
   d. A diagnosis

11. Which of the following is an alternative title for this article?

   a. Exercise and a good night's sleep
   b. Benefits of a good night's sleep
   c. Tips for a good night's sleep
   d. Lack of sleep is a serious medical condition

12. Which of the following cannot be inferred from this article?

   a. Biking is helpful for getting a good night's sleep
   b. Mental activity is helpful for getting a good night's sleep
   c. Eating bedtime snacks is not recommended
   d. Getting up at the same time is helpful for a good night's sleep

13. What is a disadvantage of taking naps?

   a. They may keep you awake.
   b. There are no disadvantages
   c. They may help you sleep better
   d. They may affect your diet

Question 14 refers to the following Table of Contents.

Contents
>Science Self-assessment 81
>Answer Key 91
>Science Tutorials 96
>Scientific Method 96
>Biology 99
>Heredity: Genes and Mutation 104
>Classification 108
>Ecology 110
>Chemistry 112
>Energy: Kinetic and Mechanical 126
>Energy: Work and Power 130
>Force: Newton's Three Laws 132

14. Consider the table of contents above. What page would you find information about natural selection and adaptation?

>a. 81
>b. 90
>c. 110
>d. 132

Questions 15 – 18 refer to the following passage.

Passage 5 - Pearl Harbour

A Day That Will Live in Infamy! Attack on Pearl Harbour
In 1941, the world was at war. The United States was trying very hard to keep itself out of the conflict. In Europe, the countries of Germany and Italy had formed an alliance to expand their land and territory. Germany had already taken over Poland, Denmark, and parts of France. They were heading next toward England and due to all the fighting in Europe, there were battles taking place as far south as North Africa, where the German and Italian armies were fighting the British.

This got even worse when the Asian nation of Japan formed

an alliance with Germany and Italy. Together, the three countries called themselves, the AXIS. Now, the war was in the Pacific as well as in Europe and Northern Africa. A great deal of Americans felt that perhaps now was the time for the United States to join with its ally, Great Britain and stop the Axis from taking over more regions of the world.

In 1941, Franklin Roosevelt was President of the United States. His fear at the time was that Japan would try to take over many countries in Asia. He did not want to see that happen, so he moved some of the United States warships that had been stationed in San Diego, to the military base at Pearl Harbor, in Honolulu, Hawaii.

Japan quietly plotted their attack. They waited until the early hours of the morning on Sunday, December 7, 1941. Then, 350 Japanese war plans began to drop bombs on the U.S. ships at Pearl Harbor. The first bombs fell at 7:48 am and a mere 90 minutes later, the attack was over. Pearl Harbor was decimated. 8 battleships were damaged. Eleven ships were sunk and 300 U.S. planes were destroyed. Most devastating was the loss of life 2,400 U.S. military members was killed in the attack and 1, 282 were injured.

President Roosevelt addressed the country via the radio and said "Today is a day that will live in infamy." He asked Congress to declare war on Japan. War was declared on Japan on December 8th and on Germany and Italy on December 11th. The United States had entered World War Two.

15. After reading the passage, what can we infer infamy means?

    a. Famous

    b. Remembered in a good way

    c. Remembered in a bad way

    d. Easily forgotten

16. What three countries formed the Axis?

    a. Italy, England, Germany

    b. United States, England, Italy

    c. Germany, Japan, Italy

    d. Germany, Japan, United States

17. What do you think was President Roosevelt's reason for moving warships to Pearl Harbor?

    a. He feared Japan would bomb San Diego

    b. He knew Japan was going to attack Pearl Harbor

    c. He was planning to attack Japan

    d. He wanted to try and protect Asian countries from Japanese takeover

18. Why do you think Japan chose a Sunday morning at 7:48 am for their attack?

    a. They knew the military slept late

    b. There is a law against bombing countries on a Sunday

    c. They wanted the attack to catch people by surprise

    d. That was the only free time they had to attack.

Questions 19 - 20 refer to the following recipe.

If You Have Allergies, You're Not Alone

People who experience allergies might joke that their immune systems have let them down or are seriously lacking. Truthfully though, people who experience allergic reactions or allergy symptoms during certain times of the year have heightened immune systems that are, "better" than those of people who have perfectly healthy but less militant immune systems.

Still, when a person has an allergic reaction, they are having an adverse reaction to a substance that is considered normal to most people. Mild allergic reactions usually have symptoms like itching, runny nose, red eyes, or bumps or discolouration of the skin. More serious allergic reactions, such as those to animal and insect poisons or certain foods, may result in the closing of the throat, swelling of the eyes, low blood pressure, inability to breath, and can even be fatal.

Different treatments help different allergies, and which one a person uses depends on the nature and severity of the allergy. It is recommended to patients with severe allergies to take extra precautions, such as carrying an EpiPen, which treats anaphylactic shock and may prevent death, always in order for the remedy to be readily available and more effective. When an allergy is not so severe, treatments may be used just relieve a person of uncomfortable symptoms. Over the counter allergy medicines treat milder symptoms, and can be bought at any grocery store and used in moderation to help people with allergies live normally.

There are many tests available to assess whether a person has allergies or what they may be allergic to, and advances in these tests and the medicine used to treat patients continues to improve. Despite this fact, allergies still affect many people throughout the year or even every day. Medicines used to treat allergies have side effects of their own, and it is difficult to bring the body into balance with the use of medicine. Regardless, many of those who live with allergies are grateful for what is available and find it useful in maintaining their lifestyles.

19. According to this passage, the word "militant" belongs in a group with the words:

    a. sickly, ailing, faint

    b. strength, power, vigour

    c. active, fighting, warring

    d. worn, tired, breaking down

20. The author says that "medicines used to treat allergies have side-effects of their own" to

   a. point out that doctors aren't very good at diagnosing and treating allergies

   b. argue that because of the large number of people with allergies, a cure will never be found

   c. explain that allergy medicines aren't cures and some compromise must be made

   d. argue that more wholesome remedies should be researched and medicines banned

Part II - Observation, Professional Judgment, Recognition and Identification.

Section I - Observation

Directions: You have five minutes to memorize the following information. Do not write anything down. Questions follow on page 163.

Name: William Jackson

Description: 5'11" Caucasian male. Brown hair with receding hairline. Slight build. No identifying marks.

Wanted for: Armed Robbery

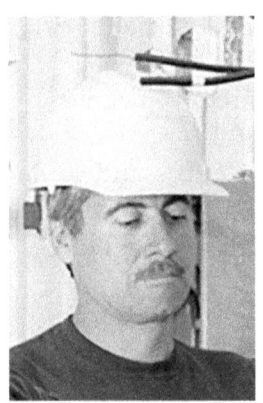

Name: Kenneth Walker

Description: 5 ft. Caucasian male with heavy build. Small scar on right forehead.

Wanted for: Armed robbery

Make: Porche Carrera

Color: White

License: Manitoba APT 936

Wanted for: Dangerous Driving

Make: Smart Car

Color: White

License: New Brunswick CPV 439

Wanted for: Criminal Harassment

Name: Steven Hermandez

Description: 6 ft Latino male with tattoos on both arms and chest.

Wanted For: Theft of motor vehicle

Name: Linda Moore

Description: 5' 4" Caucasian female, blonde hair, brown eyes, tattoos on left forearm

Wanted For: Shoplifting

Make: Volkwagen Passat

Color: White

License: British Columbia AG5 26C

Wanted for: Sexual Assault

Make: Volkswagen Beetle

Color: Yellow

License: AG5 26C

Wanted for: Sexual Assault

Section II - Professional Judgment

Scenario I

You and your partner arrive on a domestic scene where an enraged and possibly drunk or high man is destroying the furniture in a house. His wife or girlfriend is crying nearby.

1. What should you do first?

    a. Subdue the man and then report to dispatch

    b. Report to dispatch and call for backup

    c. Make sure the wife is OK

    d. Check the wife first, then subdue the man

You have confirmed the girlfriend is OK and subdued and placed the man under arrest. He has calmed down. You and your partner are preparing to take the man to the station. He begs you to release him saying it was all a big misunderstanding.

2. What should you do now?

    a. Release the man if he agrees to appear in court.

    b. Take the man to the station.

    c. Discuss what to do with your partner.

    d. Ask dispatch what to do.

Scenario II

You attend a fight in a parking lot near a popular nightclub that has just closed. You and your partner find one man with a bloody nose and looking poorly, and another man who appears to be fine. There is a crowd watching the fight.

3. What should you do?

    a. Check the injured man, keeping the men separate.

    b. Arrest both men

    c. Arrest both men and interview them separately.

    d. Check the injured man, interview both men separately.

Scenario III

4. You have just arrested a man for breaking and entering. You apprehended the suspect inside a residence with broken windows. The man tells you he will give you the name of 2 other people who recently robbed a bank in your patrol area if you let him go.

What should you do?

    a. Take down the information and let him go.

    b. Take down the information and continue with the arrest and processing.

    c. Tell him he will have to give you information about 2 or more crimes before you can let him go

    d. Call dispatch for advice.

Scenario IV

5. You have pulled over a vehicle for dangerous driving and arrested the driver. The driver of the vehicle has agreed to accompany you to the station. The driver has requested he drive his own vehicle behind yours.

What should you do?

    a. You determine the driver has not been drinking and appears calm, so you allow the driver to follow you to the station.

    b. Refuse his request and ask dispatch to call a tow truck.

    c. Question the driver more before allowing him to drive back

    d. Allow the suspect to drive his own car back with some restrictions.

Scenario V

6. You attend a call to a beach party. Nearby some cars have been vandalized. It is not clear if the people at the beach party are responsible or not, and they deny vandalizing the cars. There are 8 or 10 people at the beach party and they appear peaceful.

What should you do?

    a. Call for backup before approaching the beach party.

    b. Approach the beach party and ask if they know about the vandalized cars.

    c. Arrest everyone at the beach party.

    d. Take the names of everyone at the party.

7. Backup has arrived and you approach the beach party with 2 other officers. You are the senior officer at the scene.

What is your next step?

    a. Arrest everyone at the party

    b. Question everyone at the party about the vandalized cars

    c. Accuse everyone at the party of vandalizing the cars to see their reaction

    d. Examine the vandalized cars with the other officers.

Scenario VI

8. You have pulled over a car for speeding and are about to write up a ticket. The driver tells you he knows the mayor and the chief of police and will get you fired if you give him a ticket. He asked for your name and badge number.

What should you do?

    a. Refuse to give your name or badge.

    b. Give the driver a warning instead of a ticket

    c. Let the driver go

    d. Give your name and badge number and give him a ticket.

Scenario VII

You have attended a domestic violence call. The woman has clearly been beaten by the man, and when you enter the house, the man is breaking china and furniture.

9. What should you do first?

    a. Stop the man from further property damage.

    b. Attend the woman's injuries

    c. Call for backup

    d. Check the house for other people or children.

Scenario VIII

You are called to a robbery at a jewelry store. You arrive and the owner of the store is unconscious and the a male is exiting the store by the front door as you enter the back. The male robbery suspect is carrying a bag, which may contain jewelry from the store.

10. What should you do?

    a. Chase the robbery suspect.

    b. Check the unconscious owner

    c. Assess what has been stolen

    d. Call for backup

Section III - Recognition and Identification

11. Choose the person that matches the suspect below.

a.

b.

c.

d.

12. Choose the person that matches the suspect below.

a.    b.

c.    d.

13. Choose the person that matches the suspect below.

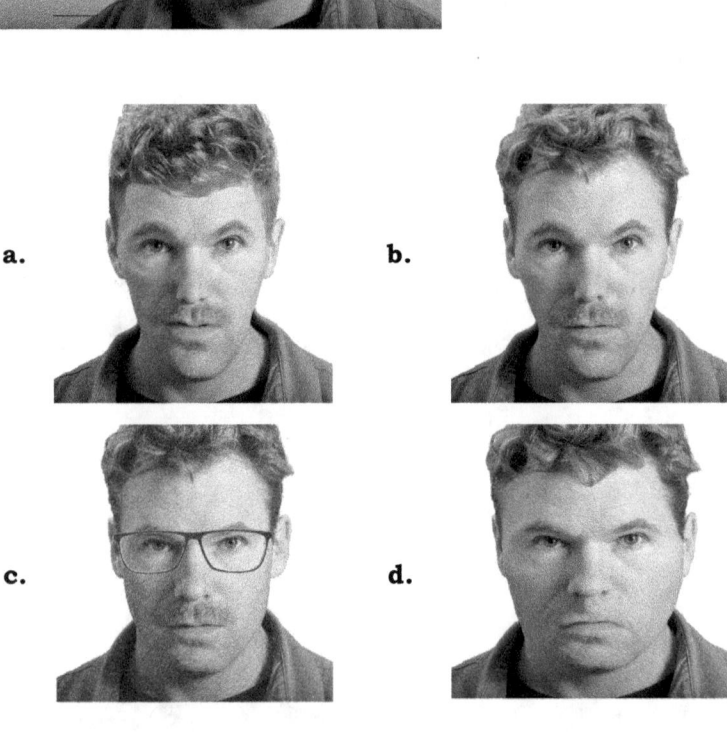

Section I - Observation Questions

Directions: Answer questions 14 - 20 based on the information given on page 33 - 37.

14. What identifying marks does Kenneth Walker have?

    a. Scar on forehead
    b. Tattoo on chest
    c. Tattoo on right arm
    d. No identifying marks

15. What is Kenneth Walker wanted for?

    a. Dangerous Driving
    b. Armed Robbery
    c. Fraud
    d. Criminal Harassment

16. Which car is wanted for Dangerous Driving?

    a. Porche Carrera
    b. Smart Car
    c. Volkwagen Passat
    d. None of the above.

17. What Province is the Smart Car from?

    a. British Columbia
    b. New Brunswick
    c. Alberta
    d. Ontario

18. What is Steven Hermandez wanted for?

    a. Theft of motor vehicle

    b. Fraud

    c. Armed Robbery

    d. Criminal Harassment

19. What identifying marks does Linda Moore have?

    a. No identifying marks

    b. Scar on forehead

    c. Tattoos on forearm

    d. Scar on upper lip

20. What color is the Volkswagen Beetle?

    a. White

    b. Yellow

    c. Red

    d. Blue

Part IV – Math

1. What is 1/3 of 3/4?

    a. 1/4
    b. 1/3
    c. 2/3
    d. 3/4

2. What fraction of $1500 is $75?

    a. 1/14
    b. 3/5
    c. 7/10
    d. 1/20

3. 3.14 + 2.73 + 23.7 =

    a. 28.57
    b. 30.57
    c. 29.56
    d. 29.57

4. A woman spent 15% of her income on an item and ends with $120. What percentage of her income is left?

    a. 12%
    b. 85%
    c. 75%
    d. 95%

5. A mother is making spaghetti for her son. The recipe that she's using says that for 500 grams of spaghetti, she should add 0.75 grams of salt. However, the mom just wants 125 grams of spaghetti. Based on this information, how much salt should she use?

    a. 0.38 grams
    b. 0.75 grams
    c. 0.19 grams
    d. 0.25 grams

6. A pet store sold $19,304.56 worth of merchandise in June. If the cost of products sold was $5,284.34, employees were paid $8,384.76, and rent was $2,920.00, how much profit did the store make in June?

    a. $5,635.46
    b. $2,714.46
    c. $14,020.22
    d. $10,019.80

7. At the beginning of 2009, Madalyn invested $5,000 in a savings account. The account pays 4% interest per year. At the end of the year, after the interest was awarded, how much did Madalyn have in the account?

    a. $5,200
    b. $5,020
    c. $5,110
    d. $7,000

8. If 144 students need to go on a trip and the buses each carry 36 students, how many buses are needed?

    a. 6
    b. 5
    c. 4
    d. 3

9. If a square if five feet tall, what is its area?

    a. 5 square feet
    b. 10 square feet
    c. 20 square feet
    d. 25 square feet

10. With a purely random guess, what are the chances of correctly guessing the month in which a person was born?

    a. 1 : 3
    b. 1 : 6
    c. 1 : 4
    d. 1 : 12

11. John is a barber and receives 40% of the amount paid by each of his customers. John gets all tips paid to him. If a man pays $8.50 for a haircut and pays a tip of $1.30, how much money goes to John?

    a. $3.92
    b. $4.70
    c. $5.30
    d. $6.40

12. Susan was surprised to find she had two more quarters than she believed she had in her purse. If quarters are the only coins, and the total is $8.75, how many quarters did she think she had?

    a. 35
    b. 29
    c. 31
    d. 33

13. There were some oranges in a basket, by adding 8/5 of these, the total became 130. How many oranges were in the basket?

    a. 60
    b. 50
    c. 40
    d. 35

14. Mr. Brown bought 5 burgers, 3 drinks, 4 fries for his family and a cookie for the dog. If the price of all single items is same, at $1.30 and a 3.5% tax is added, then what is the total cost of dinner?

    a. $16.00
    b. $16.90
    c. $17.00
    d. $17.50

15. A distributor purchased 550 kilograms of potatoes for $165. He distributed these at a rate of $6.4 per 20 kilograms to 15 shops, $3.4 per 10 kilograms to 12 shops and the remainder at $1.8 per 5 kilograms. If his total distribution cost is $10, what will his profit be?

    a. $10.40
    b. $8.60
    c. $14.90
    d. $23.40

16. Convert 3 yards to feet

    a. 18 feet
    b. 12 feet
    c. 9 feet
    d. 27 feet

17. 12t - 10 = 14t + 2. Find t

    a. -6
    b. -4
    c. 4
    d. 6

18. The price of a book went up from $20 to $25. What percent did the price increase?

    a. 5%
    b. 10%
    c. 20%
    d. 25%

19. The price of a book decreased from $25 to $20. What percent did the price decrease?

    a. 5%
    b. 10%
    c. 20%
    d. 25%

20. 305 X 25 =

    a. 6525
    b. 7625
    c. 5026
    d. 7026

Part IV - Logic

1. Consider the following sequence: 13, 26, 52, 104, ...
What number should come next?

    a. 208
    b. 106
    c. 200
    d. 400

2. Consider the following sequence: 32, 26, 20, 14, ...
What number should come next?

    a. 12
    b. 19
    c. 10
    d. 8

3. Consider the following sequence: 12, 4, 16, ..., 36.
What is the missing number?

    a. 18
    b. 22
    c. 20
    d. 30

Directions: Find the sentence that is true according to the given information.

4. Ben and Ted are classmates. They would ride the school bus together. They also have lunch at the same table. They're even lab partners.

   a. Ben and Ted don't like each other.
   b. Ben prefers being with other children.
   c. Ben and Ted are inseparable.
   d. Ted is always alone.

5. Karen takes care of her garden everyday. She grows fruits and vegetables. She always waters them. She also pulls out the weeds and put fertilizer on her plants.

   a. Karen hates taking care of her plants.
   b. Karen is fond of gardening.
   c. Karen plants flowers in her garden.
   d. Karen and her mother work on the garden together.

6. Collecting stamps is Tom's hobby. He started collecting stamps when he was six years old. Today, Tom has over a thousand stamps in his collection.

   a. Tom collects stamp albums.
   b. Tom started collecting stamps in high school.
   c. Tom is a stamp collector.
   d. Collecting stamps is an expensive hobby.

7. Mother went to market. She bought apples, oranges, and bananas. She also bought cabbage, beans, and squash.

    a. Vegetables in the market are expensive.

    b. Mother bought chicken and meat.

    c. Many people went to the market.

    d. Mother bought fruits and vegetables.

8. Tommy and Timmy are brothers. They look the same. They also have the same birthdays.

    a. Tommy is older than Timmy.

    b. Timmy is more handsome than Tommy.

    c. Tommy and Timmy are twins.

    d. Tommy and Timmy are best friends.

9. Five students exam marks are posted on a sheet at the front of the class, from lowest at the top, to highest at the bottom.

1. Peter's mark is smaller than Brad's but higher than Emily's mark.
2. Brad's mark is lower that Brittany's.
3. Andrew's mark is third.

Who got the highest mark?

    a. Emily

    b. Brad

    c. Brittany

    d. Cannot be determined.

In the code below, the following rules apply:

1. Each letter always represents the same word.
2. Each word is represented by only one letter.
3. The position of a letter and a word in the sentence are never the same.

Z	B	W	O		V		means
Linda	likes	French	lessons		best		

B	C	O		V		E	means
Peter	likes	science		lessons		best	

V	A	G	W	N	means
Linda	does	not	like	algebra	

10. What letter represents Linda?

    a. Z
    b. B
    c. W
    d. None of the above.

11. What does 'V' represent?

    a. Science
    b. Lessons
    c. Best
    d. Like

Directions: Read the following report and answer questions 12 and 13.

You come on an accident scene on Majestic Ave. A vehicle has been hit and another vehicle, with a damaged front end is fleeing the scene. The vehicle proceeds north on Majestic and turns right on Arbutus St., then left on Oak st., right on Richmond, and then right again on Birch. The vehicle stops on Birch.

12. What direction was the vehicle traveling on Arbutus?

      a. North
      b. South
      c. East
      d. West

13. What direction was the vehicle traveling on Richmond?

      a. North
      b. South
      c. East
      d. West

14. Arrange the following in the correct sequence.

a. Teens refuse to give their names
b. Several teens flee the scene
c. Dispatch reports a beach party
d. You approach a group of teens

    a. CDAB

    b. DABC

    c. ABCD

    d. ADCB

15. Arrange the following in the correct sequence.

a. Robert Smith is charged.
b. A suspect gives his name as Andrew Jones and is released.
c. The suspect is later arrested by other officers.
d. A records check reveals an person fitting his description is actually Robert Smith with a lengthy list of priors.

    a. ABCD

    b. DCBA

    c. CBDA

    d. BDCA

Answer Key

Reading Comprehension

1. A
Helen's parents hired Anne to teach Helen to communicate. Choice B is incorrect because the passage states Anne had trouble finding her way around, which means she could walk. Choice C is incorrect because you don't hire a teacher to teach someone to play. Choice D is incorrect because by age 6, if Helen had never eaten, she would have starved to death.

2. B
The correct answer because that fact is stated directly in the passage. The passage explains that Anne taught Helen to hear by allowing her to feel the vibrations in her throat.

3. A
We can infer that Anne is a patient teacher because she did not leave or lose her temper when Helen bit or hit her; she just kept trying to teach Helen. Choice B is incorrect because Anne taught Helen to read and talk. Choice C is incorrect because Anne could hear. She was partially blind, not deaf. Choice D is incorrect because it does not have to do with patience.

4. B
The passage states that it was hard for anyone but Anne to understand Helen when she spoke. Choice A is incorrect because the passage does not mention Helen spoke a foreign language. Choice C is incorrect because there is no mention of how quiet or loud Helen's voice was. Choice D is incorrect because we know from reading the passage that Helen did learn to speak.

5. D
This question tests the reader's summarization skills. The question is asking very generally about the message of the passage, and the title, "Ways Characters Communicate in

Theatre," is one indication of that. The other choices A, B, and C are all directly from the text, and therefore readers may be inclined to select one of them, but are too specific to encapsulate the entirety of the passage and its message.

6. C
This question tests the reader's grammatical skills. Choice B seems logical, but parenthesis are actually considered to be a stronger break in a sentence than commas are, and along this line of thinking, actually disrupt the sentence more.

Choices A and D make comparisons between theatre and film that are simply not made in the passage, and may or may not be true. This detail does clarify the statement that asides are most unique to theatre by adding that it is not completely unique to theatre, which may have been why the author didn't chose not to delete it and instead used parentheses to designate the detail's importance (choice C).

7. A
Low blood sugar occurs both in diabetics and healthy adults.

8. B
None of the statements are the author's opinion.

9. A
The only statement that is not a detail is, "A doctor can diagnosis this medical condition by asking the patient questions and testing."

10. A
This sentence is a recommendation.

11. C
Tips for a good night's sleep is the best alternative title for this article.

12. B
Mental activity is helpful for a good night's sleep is cannot be inferred from this article.

13. A
From the passage, one disadvantage of taking naps is they may keep you awake at night.

14. C
You would find information about natural selection and adaptation in the ecology section which begins on page 110.

15. C
To be infamous means to be remembered for an evil or terrible action. Therefore, the word infamy means to remember a bad or terrible thing. Choice A is incorrect because being famous is not the same as being infamous. Choice B is incorrect because the attack on Pearl Harbor was not good. Choice D is incorrect because Pearl Harbor was not forgotten.

16. C
Each answer choice except choice C contains the name of at least one country that was not part of the AXIS powers.

17. D
It is stated in the passage. Choice A is not correct because there was no indication that Japan would attack San Diego. Choice B is incorrect because the attack on Pearl Harbor was a surprise. Choice C is incorrect because Roosevelt was not planning to attack Japan.

18. C
The passage clearly states that Japan planned a surprise attack. They chose that early time to catch the U.S. military off guard. Choice A is incorrect because the military does not sleep late. Choice B is incorrect because there is no law against bombing countries. Choice D is incorrect because it makes no sense.

19. C
This question tests the reader's vocabulary skills. The uses of the negatives "but" and "less," especially right next to each other, may confuse readers into answering with choices A or D, which list words that are antonyms to "militant." Readers may also be confused by the comparison of healthy people with what is being described as an overly healthy person-- both people are good, but the reader may look for which one is "worse" in the comparison, and therefore stray toward the antonym words. One key to understanding the meaning of "militant" if the reader is unfamiliar with it is to look

at the root of the word; readers can then easily associate it with "military" and gain a sense of what the word signifies: defense (especially considered that the immune system defends the body). Choice C is correct over choice B because "militant" is an adjective, just as the words in choice C are, whereas the words in choice B are nouns.

20. C
This question tests the reader's understanding of function within writing. The other choices are details included surrounding the quoted text, and may therefore confuse the reader. A somewhat contradicts what is said earlier in the paragraph, which is that tests and treatments are improving, and probably doctors are along with them, but the paragraph doesn't actually mention doctors, and the subject of the question is the medicine. Choice B may seem correct to readers who aren't careful to understand that, while the author does mention the large number of people affected, the author is touching on the realities of living with allergies rather about the likelihood of curing all allergies. Similarly, while the author does mention the "balance" of the body, which is easily associated with "wholesome," the author is not really making an argument and especially is not making an extreme statement that allergy medicines should be outlawed. Again, because the article's tone is on living with allergies, choice C is an appropriate choice that fits with the title and content of the text.

Part II - Observation, Professional Judgment, Recognition and Identification.

Professional Judgment

1. D
The priority is safety, so checking the wife is the first thing, then subdue the man.

2. B
There is no reason to release the man as he has caused significant damage.

3. D
The first priority is the ensure safety, then to interview both men separately.

4. B
If the suspect is willing to provide information about another crime, then take the information, but this cannot be bartered for release after arrest.

5. B
Under no circumstances should the suspect drive his own car.

6. A
The safest course of action is the wait for backup.

7. B
The safest action is the approach the beach party and ask if they know anything about the vandalized cars, and your next response will depend on their reaction and information.

8. D
Give your name and badge number and give him a ticket.

9. B
The first objective is to assess the woman's injuries and call for an ambulance if necessary.

10. B
The first responsibility is to the unconscious owner. After, or while assessing the unconscious owner, call update dispatch of the whole situation.

Recognition and Identification

11. A
Choice A has the same face but different hair. The other suspects have much thinner, or different shaped faces.

12. C
Choice C is the same person wearing sunglasses. The suspect's face in choices A and D are much thinner and the suspect in choice B is wider.

13. C
The suspects in choices A and B have a thinner face, and the suspect in choice D has a wider face.

Observation

14. D
William Jackson does not have any identifying marks.

15. B
Kenneth Walker is wanted for armed robbery.

16. A
The Porche Carrera is wanted for dangerous driving.

17. B
The Smart Car is from New Brunswick.

18. A
Steven Hermandez is wanted for theft of a motor vehicle.

19. C
Linda Moore has tatoos on her left forearm.

20. B
The Volkwagen Beetle is yellow.

Composition

1. C
Dauntless: adj. Invulnerable to fear or intimidation.

2. A
Juxtaposed: adj. Placed side by side often for comparison or contrast.

3. B
Regicide: v. killing of a king.

4. A
Pernicious: adj. Causing much harm in a subtle way.

5. A
Immune: adj. Resistant to a particular infection or toxin owing to the presence of specific antibodies.

6. B
Nimble: adj. Quick and light in movement or action. Agile.

7. A
Queries: n. Questions or inquiries.

8. C
Depose: To remove (a leader) from (high) office, without killing the incumbent.

9. D
Pedestrian: Ordinary, dull; everyday; unexceptional.

10. B
Petulant: adj. Childishly irritable.

11. C
Humorous is the correct spelling.

12. B
Knowledge is the correct spelling.

13. A
Camaraderie is the correct spelling.

14. A
Mathematics is the correct spelling.

15. C
Conscientious is the correct spelling.

16. D
Leisure is the correct spelling.

17. C
Pigeon is the correct spelling.

18. D
Odyssey is the correct spelling.

19. C
Sacrilegious is the correct spelling.

20. A
Accommodate is the correct spelling.

21. C
The major words in the titles of books, articles, and songs are capitalized. (but not short prepositions or the articles "the," "a," or "an," if they are not the first word of the title)

22. A
Titles of publications are capitalized.

23. A
Singular subjects. "The Chinese" is plural, and "a citizen of Bermuda" is singular.

24. A
Disease is singular.

25. C
Articles of speech. Both dog and cat in this sentence are singular and require the article 'a.'

26. B
Former vs. Latter. 'Former' refers to the first of two things, 'latter' to the second.

27. B
Fewer vs. Less. 'Fewer' is used with countables and 'less' is used with un-countables.

28. A
'However' usage. 'However' usually has a comma before and after.

29. D
'However' Usage. 'However' usually has a comma before and after.

30. A
The third conditional is used for talking about an unreal situation (that did not happen) in the past. For example, "If I had studied harder, [if clause] I would have passed the exam [main clause]. Which is the same as, "I failed the exam, because I didn't study hard enough."

Part IV – Mathematics

1. A
1/3 X 3/4 = 3/12 = 1/4

2. D
75/1500 = 15/300 = 3/60 = 1/20

3. D
3.14 + 2.73 = 5.87 and 5.87 + 23.7 = 29.57

4. B
Spent 15% - 100% - 15% = 85%

5. C
125 : 500 is the same as 25 : 100 or 1 : 4. So the amount of salt will be 0.75/4 = 0.1875, or about .19 grams.

6. B
Total expenses = 5284.34 + $8,384.76 + $2,920.00 = $16,589.10

Profit = revenue less expenses

$19,304.56 - 16589.10 = $2,715.46

7. A
$5,000 at 4% = 5000 X 4/100
5000 X .4 = 200
So the total after one year will be $5,200

8. C
If each bus carries 36 students, and there are 144 students total, then 144/36 = 4 buses.

9. D
If a square is 5 feet tall, then the area will be 5 X 5 = 25.

10. D
Since there are 12 months in a year = 12 possibilities, the chance of guessing the correct month will be 1 in 12.

11. B
John's total will be 40% of 8.50 plus the tip of $1.30.

8.5 X 4/100 = 8.5 X .4 = 3.40

Total = 3.40 + 1.30 = $4.70.

12. D
If she has $8.75, that will equal 35 quarters. ($8.00 = 32 quarters and $.75 = 3 quarters, total 35 quarters).

She had 2 more quarters than she thought, so she had 35 - 2 = 33 quarters.

13. B
Suppose oranges in the basket before = x, Then: X + 8x/5 = 130, 5x + 8x = 650, so X = 50.

14. D
As price of all the single items is same and there are 13 total items. So the total cost will be 13 × 1.3 = $16.90. After 3.5 percent tax this amount will become 16.9×1.035=$17.50.

15. B
The distribution is done in three different rates and amounts:

$6.4 per 20 kilograms to 15 shops ... 20•15 = 300 kilograms distributed

$3.4 per 10 kilograms to 12 shops ... 10•12 = 120 kilograms distributed

550 - (300 + 120) = 550 - 420 = 130 kilograms left. This amount is distributed by 5 kilogram portions. So, this means that there are 130/5 = 26 shops.

$1.8 per 130 kilograms.

We need to find the amount he earned overall these distributions.

$6.4 per 20 kilograms : 6.4•15 = $96 for 300 kilograms

$3.4 per 10 kilograms : 3.4•12 = $40.8 for 120 kilograms

$1.8 per 5 kilograms : 1.8•26 = $46.8 for 130 kilograms

So, he earned 96 + 40.8 + 46.8 = $ 183.6

The total distribution cost is given as $10

The profit is found by: Money earned - money spent ... It is important to remember that he bought 550 kilograms of potatoes for $165 at the beginning:

Profit = 183.6 - 10 - 165 = $8.6

16. C
1 yard = 3 feet, 3 yards = 3 feet x 3 = 9 feet

17. C
12t -10 = 14t + 2

Collect terms with the same variable on the same side, switching to negative if you bring terms over the equals sign.

-2t - 10 = 2

Collect number on the same side switching to negative if you bring terms over the equals sign.

-2t = -8

Divide both sides by -2.
-t = -4
t = 4

18. D
Price increased by $5 ($25-$20). The percent increase is 5/20 x 100 = 5 x 5 = 25%

19. C
Price decreased by $5 ($25-$20). The percent increase = 5/25 x 100 = 5 x 4 = 20%

20. B
305 X 25 = 7625

Part V - Logic

1. A
The number doubles each time.

2. D
The numbers decrease by 6 each time.

3. C
Each number is the sum of the previous two numbers.

4. C

The only certain thing is Ben and Ted are inseparable.

5. B

The only certain thing is Karen is fond of gardening.

6. C

The only certain thing is Tom is a stamp collector.

7. D

The only certain thing is mother bought fruits and vegetables.

8. C

The only certain thing is they are twins.

9. C

Brittany's mark is the highest.

According to condition 1, the order is:

Emily
Peter
Brad

With condition 2,

Emily
Peter
Brad
Brittany

With condition 3,

Emily
Peter
Andrew
Brad
Brittany

The list is from lowest at the top to highest at the bottom, so Brittany's mark is the highest.

10. C
Linda appears in the first and third sentence and so do 'Z' and 'W,' so it must be one of the two. 'Z' is in the same position as Linda in the first sentence and can be eliminated, so Linda must be 'W.'

11. D
'Like' is in all three sentences, so it must be 'B,' 'O' or 'V.' The only one of these three to appear in the third sentence is 'V,' so it must be 'like.'

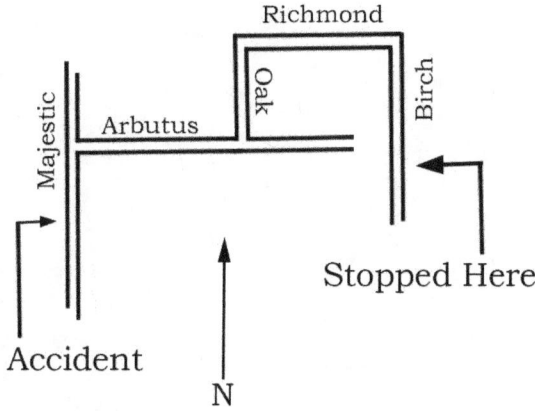

12. C
The vehicle was traveling east on Arbutus.

13. C
The vehicle was traveling east on Richmond.

14. A
C, D, A, B is the correct sequence.

> c. Dispatch reports a beach party
> d. You approach a group of teens
> a. Teens refuse to give their names
> b. Several teens flee the scene

15. D
B, D, C, A is the correct sequence.

> b. A suspect gives his name as Andrew Jones and is released.
>
> d. A records check reveals an person fitting his description is actually Robert Smith with a lengthy list of priors.
>
> c. The suspect is later arrested by other officers.
> a. Robert Smith is charged.

Practice Test Questions Set 2

The questions below are not the same as you will find on the RCMP - that would be too easy! And nobody knows what the questions will be and they change all the time. Below are general questions that cover the same subject areas as the RCMP. So the format and exact wording of the questions may differ slightly, and change from year to year, if you can answer the questions below, you will have no problem with the RCMP.

For the best results, take these Practice Test Questions as if it were the real exam. Set aside time when you will not be disturbed, and a location that is quiet and free of distractions. Read the instructions carefully, read each question carefully, and answer to the best of your ability.
Use the bubble answer sheets provided. When you have completed the Practice Questions, check your answer against the Answer Key and read the explanation provided.

Do not attempt more than one set of practice test questions in one day. After completing the first practice test, wait two or three days before attempting the second set of questions.

Reading Comprehension - 20 Questions

Observation – 7 Questions

Professional Judgment: 10 Questions

Recognition/Identification – 3 Questions

Composition – 20 questions

Math - 20 questions

Logic – 20 questions

Reading Comprehension

	A	B	C	D
1	○	○	○	○
2	○	○	○	○
3	○	○	○	○
4	○	○	○	○
5	○	○	○	○
6	○	○	○	○
7	○	○	○	○
8	○	○	○	○
9	○	○	○	○
10	○	○	○	○
11	○	○	○	○
12	○	○	○	○
13	○	○	○	○
14	○	○	○	○
15	○	○	○	○
16	○	○	○	○
17	○	○	○	○
18	○	○	○	○
19	○	○	○	○
20	○	○	○	○

Observation, Professional Judgment, Recognition and Identification

	A	B	C	D
1	○	○	○	○
2	○	○	○	○
3	○	○	○	○
4	○	○	○	○
5	○	○	○	○
6	○	○	○	○
7	○	○	○	○
8	○	○	○	○
9	○	○	○	○
10	○	○	○	○
11	○	○	○	○
12	○	○	○	○
13	○	○	○	○
14	○	○	○	○
15	○	○	○	○
16	○	○	○	○
17	○	○	○	○
18	○	○	○	○
19	○	○	○	○
20	○	○	○	○

Composition

	A	B	C	D
1	○	○	○	○
2	○	○	○	○
3	○	○	○	○
4	○	○	○	○
5	○	○	○	○
6	○	○	○	○
7	○	○	○	○
8	○	○	○	○
9	○	○	○	○
10	○	○	○	○
11	○	○	○	○
12	○	○	○	○
13	○	○	○	○
14	○	○	○	○
15	○	○	○	○
16	○	○	○	○
17	○	○	○	○
18	○	○	○	○
19	○	○	○	○
20	○	○	○	○

Math

	A	B	C	D
1	○	○	○	○
2	○	○	○	○
3	○	○	○	○
4	○	○	○	○
5	○	○	○	○
6	○	○	○	○
7	○	○	○	○
8	○	○	○	○
9	○	○	○	○
10	○	○	○	○
11	○	○	○	○
12	○	○	○	○
13	○	○	○	○
14	○	○	○	○
15	○	○	○	○
16	○	○	○	○
17	○	○	○	○
18	○	○	○	○
19	○	○	○	○
20	○	○	○	○

Logic

	A	B	C	D
1	○	○	○	○
2	○	○	○	○
3	○	○	○	○
4	○	○	○	○
5	○	○	○	○
6	○	○	○	○
7	○	○	○	○
8	○	○	○	○
9	○	○	○	○
10	○	○	○	○
11	○	○	○	○
12	○	○	○	○
13	○	○	○	○
14	○	○	○	○
15	○	○	○	○
16	○	○	○	○
17	○	○	○	○
18	○	○	○	○
19	○	○	○	○
20	○	○	○	○

Reading Comprehension

Questions 1 - 3 refer to the following passage.

Passage 1 - The Crusades

In 1095 Pope Urban II proclaimed the First Crusade with the intent and stated goal to restore Christian access to holy places in and around Jerusalem. Over the next 200 years there were 6 major crusades and numerous minor crusades in the fight for control of the "Holy Land." Historians are divided on the real purpose of the Crusades, some believing that it was part of a purely defensive war against Islamic conquest; some see them as part of a long-running conflict at the frontiers of Europe; and others see them as confident, aggressive, papal-led expansion attempts by Western Christendom. The impact of the crusades was profound, and judgment of the Crusaders ranges from laudatory to highly critical. However, all agree that the Crusades and wars waged during those crusades were brutal and often bloody. Several hundred thousand Roman Catholic Christians joined the Crusades, they were Christians from all over Europe.

Europe at the time was under the Feudal System, so while the Crusaders made vows to the Church they also were beholden to their Feudal Lords. This led to the Crusaders not only fighting the Saracen, the commonly used word for Muslim at the time, but also each other for power and economic gain in the Holy Land. This infighting between the Crusaders is why many historians hold the view that the Crusades were simply a front for Europe to invade the Holy Land for economic gain in the name of the Church. Another factor contributing to this theory is that while the army of crusaders marched towards Jerusalem they pillaged the land as they went. The church and feudal Lords vowing to return the land to its original beauty, and inhabitants, this rarely happened though as the Lords often kept the land for themselves. A full 800 years after the Crusades, Pope John Paul II expressed his sorrow for the massacre of innocent people and the lasting damage the Medieval church caused in that area of the World.

1. What can all historians agree on concerning the Crusades?

   a. It achieved great things
   b. It stabilized the Holy Land
   c. It was bloody and brutal
   d. It helped defend Europe from the Byzantine Empire

2. What impact did the feudal system have on the Crusades?

   a. It unified the Crusaders
   b. It helped gather volunteers
   c. It had no effect on the Crusades
   d. It led to infighting, causing more damage than good

3. What does Saracen mean?

   a. Muslim
   b. Christian
   c. Knight
   d. Holy Land

Questions 4 - 7 refer to the following passage.

ABC Electric Warranty

ABC Electric Company warrants that its products are free from defects in material and workmanship. Subject to the conditions and limitations set forth below, ABC Electric will, at its option, either repair or replace any part of its products that prove defective due to improper workmanship or materials.

This limited warranty does not cover any damage to the product from improper installation, accident, abuse, misuse, natural disaster, insufficient or excessive electrical supply, abnormal mechanical or environmental conditions, or any unauthorized disassembly, repair, or modification.

This limited warranty also does not apply to any product on which the original identification information has been altered, or removed, has not been handled or packaged correctly, or has been sold as second-hand.

This limited warranty covers only repair, replacement, refund or credit for defective ABC Electric products, as provided above.

4. I tried to repair my ABC Electric blender, but could not, so can I get it repaired under this warranty?

    a. Yes, the warranty still covers the blender

    b. No, the warranty does not cover the blender

    c. Uncertain. ABC Electric may or may not cover repairs under this warranty

5. My ABC Electric fan is not working. Will ABC Electric provide a new one or repair this one?

    a. ABC Electric will repair my fan

    b. ABC Electric will replace my fan

    c. ABC Electric could either replace or repair my fan can request either a replacement or a repair.

6. My stove was damaged in a flood. Does this warranty cover my stove?

    a. Yes, it is covered.

    b. No, it is not covered.

    c. It may or may not be covered.

    d. ABC Electric will decide if it is covered

7. Which of the following is an example of improper workmanship?

   a. Missing parts
   b. Defective parts
   c. Scratches on the front
   d. None of the above

Questions 8 – 11 refer to the following passage.

Passage 2 - Women and Advertising

Only in the last few generations have media messages been so widespread and so readily seen, heard, and read by so many people. Advertising is an important part of both selling and buying anything from soap to cereal to jeans. For whatever reason, more consumers are women than are men. Media message are subtle but powerful, and more attention has been paid lately to how these message affect women. Of all the products that women buy, makeup, clothes, and other stylistic or cosmetic products are among the most popular. This means that companies focus their advertising on women, promising them that their product will make her feel, look, or smell better than the next company's product will. This competition has resulted in advertising that is more and more ideal and less and less possible for everyday women. However, because women do look to these ideals and the products they represent as how they can potentially become, many women have developed unhealthy attitudes about themselves when they have failed to become those ideals.

In recent years, more companies have tried to change advertisements to be healthier for women. This includes featuring models of more sizes and addressing a huge outcry against unfair tools such as airbrushing and photo editing. There is debate about what the right balance between real and ideal is, because fashion is also considered art and some changes are made to purposefully elevate fashionable products and signify that they are creative, innovative, and the work of individual people. Artists want their freedom protected as much as women do, and advertising agencies are often caught in the middle.

Some claim that the companies who make these changes are not doing enough. Many people worry that there are still not enough models of different sizes and different ethnicities. Some people claim that companies use this healthier type of advertisement not for the good of women, but because they would like to sell products to the women who are looking for these kinds of messages. This is also a hard balance to find: companies do need to make money, and women do need to feel respected.

While the focus of this change has been on women, advertising can also affect men, and this change will hopefully be a lesson on media for all consumers.

8. The second paragraph states that advertising focuses on women

    a. to shape what the ideal should be

    b. because women buy makeup

    c. because women are easily persuaded

    d. because of the types of products that women buy

9. According to the passage, fashion artists and female consumers are at odds because

    a. there is a debate going on and disagreement drives people apart

    b. both of them are trying to protect their freedom to do something

    c. artists want to elevate their products above the reach of women

    d. women are creative, innovative, individual people

10. The author uses the phrase "for whatever reason" in this passage to

   a. keep the focus of the paragraph on media messages and not on the differences between men and women

   b. show that the reason for this is unimportant

   c. argue that it is stupid that more women are consumers than men

   d. show that he or she is tired of talking about why media messages are important

11. This passage suggests that

   a. advertising companies are still working on making their messages better

   b. all advertising companies seek to be more approachable for women

   c. women are only buying from companies that respect them

   d. artists could stop producing fashionable products if they feel bullied

Questions 12 - 15 refer to the following passage.

FDR, the Treaty of Versailles, and the Fourteen Points

At the conclusion of World War I, those who had won the war and those who were forced to admit defeat welcomed the end of the war and expected that a peace treaty would be signed. The American president, Franklin D. Roosevelt, played an important part in proposing what the agreements should be and did so through his Fourteen Points.
World War I had begun in 1914 when an Austrian archduke was assassinated, leading to a domino effect that pulled the world's most powerful countries into war on a large scale. The war catalyzed the creation and use of deadly weapons that had not previously existed, resulting in a great loss of soldiers on both sides of the fighting. More than 9 million soldiers were killed.

The United States agreed to enter the war right before it ended, and many believed that its decision to become finally involved brought on the end of the war. FDR made it very clear that the U.S. was entering the war for moral reasons and had an agenda focused on world peace. The Fourteen Points were individual goals and ideas (focused on peace, free trade, open communication, and self reliance) that FDR wanted the power nations to strive for now that the war had concluded. He was optimistic and had many ideas about what could be accomplished through and during the post-war peace. However, FDR's fourteen points were poorly received when he presented them to the leaders of other world powers, many of whom wanted only to help their own countries and to punish the Germans for fueling the war, and they fell by the wayside. World War II was imminent, for Germany lost everything.

Some historians believe that the other leaders who participated in the Treaty of Versailles weren't receptive to the Fourteen Points because World War I was fought almost entirely on European soil, and the United States lost much less than did the other powers. FDR was in a unique position to determine the fate of the war, but doing it on his own terms did not help accomplish his goals. This is only one historical example of how the United State has tried to use its power as an important country, but found itself limited because of geological or ideological factors.

12. The main idea of this passage is that

a. World War I was unfair because no fighting took place in America

b. World War II happened because of the Treaty of Versailles

c. the power the United States has to help other countries also prevents it from helping other countries

d. Franklin D. Roosevelt was one of the United States' smartest presidents

13. According to the second paragraph, World War I started because

a. an archduke was assassinated

b. weapons that were more deadly had been developed

c. a domino effect of allies agreeing to help each other

d. the world's most powerful countries were large

14. The author includes the detail that 9 million soldiers were killed

a. to demonstrate why European leaders were hesitant to accept peace

b. to show the reader the dangers of deadly weapons

c. to make the reader think about which countries lost the most soldiers

d. to demonstrate why World War II was imminent

15. According to this passage, the word catalyzed means

a. analyzed

b. sped up

c. invented

d. funded

Questions 16 - 19 refer to the following passage.

Chocolate Chip Cookies

3/4 cup sugar
3/4 cup packed brown sugar
1 cup butter, softened
2 large eggs, beaten
1 teaspoon vanilla extract
2 1/4 cups all-purpose flour
1 teaspoon baking soda
3/4 teaspoon salt
2 cups semisweet chocolate chips

If desired, 1 cup chopped pecans, or chopped walnuts. Preheat oven to 375 degrees.

Mix sugar, brown sugar, butter, vanilla and eggs in a large bowl. Stir in flour, baking soda, and salt. The dough will be very stiff.

Stir in chocolate chips by hand with a sturdy wooden spoon. Add the pecans, or other nuts, if desired. Stir until the chocolate chips and nuts are evenly dispersed.

Drop dough by rounded tablespoonfuls 2 inches apart onto a cookie sheet.

Bake 8 to 10 minutes or until light brown. Cookies may look underdone, but they will finish cooking after you take them out of the oven.

16. What is the correct order for adding these ingredients?

    a. Brown sugar, baking soda, chocolate chips

    b. Baking soda, brown sugar, chocolate chips

    c. Chocolate chips, baking soda, brown sugar

    d. Baking soda, chocolate chips, brown sugar

17. What does sturdy mean?

    a. Long

    b. Strong

    c. Short

    d. Wide

18. What does disperse mean?

   a. Scatter
   b. To form a ball
   c. To stir
   d. To beat

19. When can you stop stirring the nuts?

   a. When the cookies are cooked.
   b. When the nuts are evenly distributed.
   c. When the nuts are added.
   d. After the chocolate chips are added.

Questions 20 refers to the following passage.

Passage 5 - Frankenstein

Great God! What a scene has just taken place! I am yet dizzy with the remembrance of it. I hardly know whether I shall have the power to detail it; yet the tale which I have recorded would be incomplete without this final and wonderful catastrophe. I entered the cabin where lay the remains of my ill-fated and admirable friend. Over him hung a form which I cannot find words to describe—gigantic in stature, yet uncouth and distorted in its proportions. As he hung over the coffin, his face was concealed by long locks of ragged hair; but one vast hand was extended, in color and apparent texture like that of a mummy. When he heard the sound of my approach, he ceased to utter exclamations of grief and horror and sprung towards the window. Never did I behold a vision so horrible as his face, of such loathsome yet appalling hideousness. I shut my eyes involuntarily and endeavored to recollect what were my duties with regard to this destroyer. I called on him to stay.

He paused, looking on me with wonder, and again turning towards the lifeless form of his creator, he seemed to forget my presence, and every feature and gesture seemed instigated by the wildest rage of some uncontrollable passion.

"That is also my victim!" he exclaimed. "In his murder my crimes are consummated; the miserable series of my being is wound to its close! Oh, Frankenstein! Generous and self-devoted being! What does it avail that I now ask thee to pardon me? I, who irretrievably destroyed thee by destroying all thou lovedst. Alas! He is cold, he cannot answer me."

His voice seemed suffocated, and my first impulses, which had suggested to me the duty of obeying the dying request of my friend in destroying his enemy, were now suspended by a mixture of curiosity and compassion. I approached this tremendous being; I dared not again raise my eyes to his face, there was something so scaring and unearthly in his ugliness. I attempted to speak, but the words died away on my lips. The monster continued to utter wild and incoherent self-reproaches. At length I gathered resolution to address him in a pause of the tempest of his passion.

"Your repentance," I said, "is now superfluous. If you had listened to the voice of conscience and heeded the stings of remorse before you had urged your diabolical vengeance to this extremity, Frankenstein would yet have lived." [7]

20. Who is the "ill-fated and admirable friend" who is lying in the coffin?

    a. Frankenstein's monster

    b. Frankenstein

    c. Mary Shelley

    d. Unknown

Part II - Observation, Professional Judgment, Recognition and Identification

Directions: You have five minutes to memorize the following information. Do not write anything down. Questions follow on page 228.

Name: Janet Benoit

Description: Caucasian female with shoulder length hair. Heart tattoo on right arm.

Wanted for: Child neglect

Name: Robby Valence

Description: 5 ft 5 in Caucasian male, stocky build, no identifying marks

Wanted for: Armed Robbery

Make and Model: Volkswagen Passat

License: British Columbia MN1 23C

Wanted in Connection with: Dangerous Driving

Make and Model: Volkswagen Phaeton

License: Ontario MUYR-123

Wanted in Connection with: Fraud

Name: Nathan Abraham

Description: Black Canadian Male, 5 ft 1 in. no identifying features

Wanted for: Domestic Assault

Name: Jeffrey Crisp

Description: 5 ft 6 in Caucasian male, slight build, no identifying marks

Wanted for: Sexual Assault

Make and Model: Modified Honda Accord

License: Quebec A12 BRP

Wanted for: Homicide

Make and Model: Modified Chevrolet Truck

License: Yukon RTJ12

Wanted in Connection with: Uttering Threats

Professional Judgment

Scenario: You are called to a robbery and see two cars leaving the scene at high speed. You give chase, however, the cars are driving at very high speed and driving very dangerously.

1. What should you do?

    a. Call dispatch with as much information as possible

    b. Follow the cars and match their speed.

    c. Follow the cars at a high but safe speed, even if you fall behind

    d. Follow the cars but do not exceed the speed limit.

Scenario: You are in a meeting with several colleagues from a neighboring municipality, discussing the events of last night. A radio call comes in reporting an officer needing assistance. The location is very close to your station.

2. What should you do?

    a. Continue with the meeting as others officers will respond.

    b. Leave the meeting immediately and respond to the call

    c. Invite the other officers to respond to the call with you

    d. Wrap up the meeting early and respond to the call

Scenario: You attend a noise complaint and are questioning several teenagers. They have numerous chocolate bars in their pockets and there are chocolate bar wrappers on the ground around them. The teenagers refuse to speak with you unless you arrest them.

3. What should you do?

    a. Call the station and ask if there has been any thefts nearby

    b. Arrest the teenagers

    c. Demand that they provide you with their names

    d. Accuse them of stealing the chocolate bars

Scenario: You are on your lunch break in a local restaurant with your partner. A person approaches you in a panic saying there is a man having a heart attack in the next building.

4. What should you do?

    a. Politely tell the person you are having lunch but will radio in the call.

    b. Leave lunch immediately and investigate the report

    c. Finish you lunch and tell your junior partner to attend to the complaint

    d. Ignore the complaint

Scenario: You apprehend a black suspect apparently leaving the scene of a break and enter. The suspect accuses you of racial profiling.

5. What should you do?

    a. Release the suspect to avoid an ugly scene

    b. Deny the accusation and continue

    c. Explain that you have found him apparently leaving the scene of a crime and would like to ask some questions

    d. Explain the police policy on racial profiling

The black suspect still insists that you are stopping his because of his race and refuses to answer any questions.

What should you do?

    a. You have already explained that you have found him at the scene of a break and enter, and would like to ask some questions. The next step is to explain that if he continues to refuse, you will have to take him to the station for questioning.

    b. Arrest him immediately

    c. Explain the situation again

    d. Avoid an ugly scene and allow him to go

Scenario: You are patrolling a local street and find a couple having a heated argument.

7. What should you do?

    a. Tell the couple to stop arguing

    b. Ask if everything is OK

    c. Listen to the argument and try to resolve

    d. Listen to the argument and take the side of the best argument

Recognition and Identification

8. Choose the person that matches the suspect below.

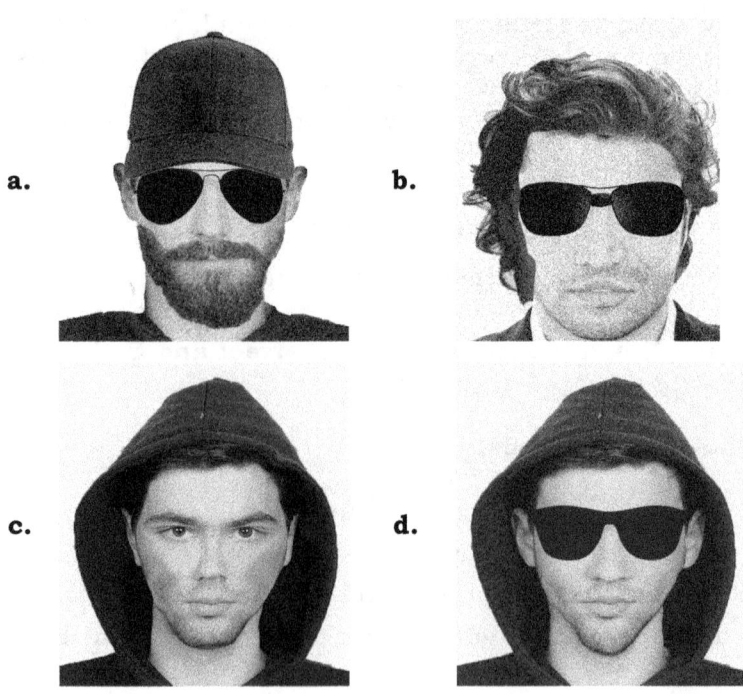

9. Choose the person that matches the suspect below.

a.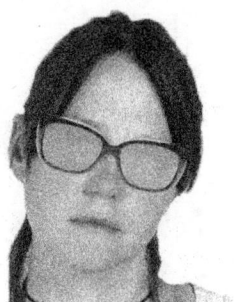

b.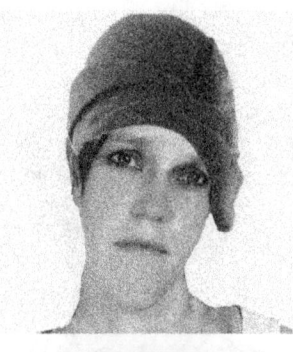

c.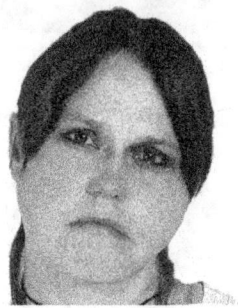

d.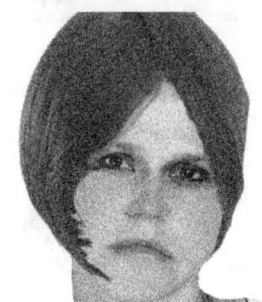

10. Choose the person that matches the suspect below.

a. 　　b.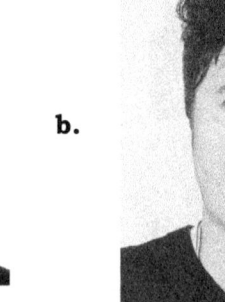

c. 　　d.

Observation

Questions 11 - 15 refer to the information on pages 91 - 94.

11. Who is wanted for child neglect?

    a. Robby Valence
    b. Janet Benoit
    c. Jeffrey Crisp
    d. Nathan Abraham

12. Who is wanted for sexual assault?

    a. Robby Valence
    b. Janet Benoit
    c. Jeffrey Crisp
    d. Nathan Abraham

13. What province is the Volkswagen Phaeton from?

    a. Yukon
    b. Quebec
    c. Ontario
    c. British Columbia

14. What is Nathan Abraham wanted for?

    a. Sexual Assault
    b. Armed Robbery
    c. Child Neglect
    d. Domestic Assault

15. What province is the modified Chevrolet truck from?

    a. Yukon

    b. Quebec

    c. Ontario

    c. British Columbia

Part III - Composition

1. Choose the best definition of anecdote.

    a. A short account of an incident

    b. Something that comes before

    c. The use of humor, irony, exaggeration, or ridicule

    d. Constant fluctuations

2. Choose the adjective that means shocking, terrible or wicked.

    a. Pleasantries

    b. Heinous

    c. Shrewd

    d. Provincial

3. Choose the noun that means a person or thing that tells or announces the coming of someone or something.

    a. Harbinger

    b. Evasion

    c. Bleak

    d. Craven

4. Choose a word that means the same as the underlined word.

He wasn't especially generous. All the servings were very <u>judicious</u>.

    a. Abundant
    b. Careful
    c. Extravagant
    d. Careless

5. Fill in the blank.

Because of the growing use of _____ as a fuel, corn production has greatly increased.

    a. Alcohol
    b. Ethanol
    c. Natural gas
    d. Oil

6. Fill in the blank.

In heavily industrialized areas, the pollution of the air causes many to develop _____ diseases.

    a. Respiratory
    b. Cardiac
    c. Alimentary
    d. Circulatory

7. Choose the best definition of inherent.

    a. To receive money in a will
    b. An essential part of
    c. To receive money from a will
    d. None of the above

8. Choose the best definition of vapid.

    a. adj. tasteless or bland

    b. v. To inflict, as a revenge or punishment

    c. v. to convert into gas

    d. v. to go up in smoke

9. Choose the best definition of waif.

    a. n. a sick and hungry child

    b. n. an orphan staying in a foster home

    c. n. homeless child or stray

    d. n. a type of French bread eaten with cheese

10. Choose the adjective that means similar or identical.

    a. Soluble

    b. Assembly

    c. Conclave

    d. Homologous

11. Choose the correct spelling.

    a. Correspondence

    b. Corespodence

    c. Correspodence

    d. Correspomdence

12. Choose the correct spelling.

    a. Henmorrhage

    b. Hemmorrhage

    c. Hemorrhage

    d. Hemorhage

13. Choose the correct spelling.

   a. Enviromnment
   b. Environment
   c. Environiment
   d. Enviromment

14. Choose the correct spelling.

   a. Govermment
   b. Goverment
   c. Govenment
   d. Government

15. Choose the correct spelling.

   a. Conceeve
   b. Concieve
   c. Conceive
   d. Conceve

16. Choose the correct spelling.

   a. Describe
   b. Decribe
   c. Decsribe
   d. Discribe

17. Choose the correct spelling.

   a. Liqour
   b. Liquor
   c. Liquer
   d. Liquour

18. Choose the correct spelling.

 a. Succesful
 b. Sucessful
 c. Sucessfull
 d. Successful

19. Choose the correct spelling.

 a. Huricane
 b. Hurricane
 c. Huricane
 d. Hurriccane

20. Choose the correct spelling.

 a. Precede
 b. Preccede
 c. Precceed
 d. Preceed

21. Choose the sentence below with the correct punctuation.

 a. There are many species of owls, the Great-Horned Owl, the Snowy Owl, and the Western Screech Owl, and the Barn Owl.

 b. There are many species of owls, the Great-Horned Owl: the Snowy Owl: and the Western Screech Owl, and the Barn Owl.

 c. There are many species of owls: the Great-Horned Owl, the Snowy Owl, and the Western Screech Owl, and the Barn Owl.

 d. There are many species of owls: the Great-Horned Owl, the Snowy Owl, and the Western Screech Owl, and the Barn Owl.

22. Choose the sentence below with the correct punctuation.

a. In his most famous speech, Reverend King proclaimed: "I have a dream!"

b. In his most famous speech, Reverend King proclaimed; "I have a dream!"

c. In his most famous speech, Reverend King proclaimed. "I have a dream!"

d. In his most famous speech: Reverend King proclaimed, "I have a dream!"

23. Choose the sentence below with the correct punctuation.

a. Puzzled — Joe said, "You aren't going to pay me until ?"

b. Puzzled, Joe said, "You aren't going to pay me until ?"

c. Puzzled, Joe said, "You aren't going to pay me until —?"

d. Puzzled, Joe said, "You aren't going to pay me until, ?"

24. Choose the sentence with the correct usage.

a. Vegetables are a healthy food; eating them can make you more healthful.

b. Vegetables are a healthful food; eating them can make you more healthful.

c. Vegetables are a healthy food; eating them can make you more healthy.

d. Vegetables are a healthful food; eating them can make you more healthy.

25. Choose the sentence with the correct usage.

a. When James went into his room, he found that his clothes had been put in the closet.

b. When James went in his room, he found that his clothes had been put in the closet.

c. When James went into his room, he found that his clothes had been put into the closet.

d. When James went in his room, he found that his clothes had been put into the closet.

26. Choose the sentence with the correct usage.

a. After you lay the books on the counter, you may lay down for a nap.

b. After you lie the books on the counter, you may lay down for a nap.

c. After you lay the books on the counter, you may lie down for a nap.

d. After you lay the books on the counter, you may lay down for a nap.

27. Choose the sentence with the correct usage.

a. He did not have to loose the race; if only his shoes weren't so lose!

b. He did not have to lose the race; if only his shoes weren't so loose!

c. He did not have to loose the race; if only his shoes weren't so lose!

d. He did not have to lose the race; if only his shoes weren't so lose!

28. Choose the sentence with the correct usage.

a. The attorney did not want to prosecute the defendant; his goal was to prosecute the guilty party.

b. The attorney did not want to persecute the defendant; his goal was to persecute the guilty party.

c. The attorney did not want to prosecute the defendant; his goal was to persecute the guilty party.

d. The attorney did not want to persecute the defendant; his goal was to prosecute the guilty party.

29. Choose the sentence with the correct usage.

a. The speeches must precede the election; the election cannot proceed without hearing from the candidates.

b. The speeches must precede the election; the election cannot precede without hearing from the candidates.

c. The speeches must proceed the election; the election cannot precede without hearing from the candidates.

d. The speeches must proceed the election; the election cannot proceed without hearing from the candidates.

30. Choose the sentence with the correct usage.

a. Before a lawyer can rise an objection, he must first rise to his feet.

b. Before a lawyer can raise an objection, he must first raise to his feet.

c. Before a lawyer can raise an objection, he must first rise to his feet.

d. Before a lawyer can rise an objection, he must first raise to his feet.

Part IV – Math

1. Estimate 2009 x 108.

    a. 110,000
    b. 2,0000
    c. 21,000
    d. 210,000

2. Richard sold 12 shirts for total revenue of $336 at 8% profit. What is the purchase price of each shirt?

    a. $25.76
    b. $24.50
    c. $23.75
    d. $22.50

3. Calculate (3a + 4b) * d when A = 2, b = 4 and d = 8

    a. 40
    b. 150
    c. 112
    d. 176

4. c = 4, n = 5 and x = 3. Calculate 2cnx/2n

    a. 12
    b. 50
    c. 8
    d. 21

5. If a = 12 and b = 8, solve 6b - a + 2a

    a. 12/9
    b. 18
    c. 16
    d. 12

6. Solve $\sqrt{121}$

    a. 11
    b. 12
    c. 21
    d. None of the above

7. In a local election at polling station A, 945 voters cast their vote out of 1270 registered voters. At polling station B, 860 cast their vote out of 1050 registered voters and at station C, 1210 cast their vote out of 1440 registered voters. What was the total turnout including all three polling stations?

    a. 70%
    b. 74%
    c. 76%
    d. 80%

8. In a factory, the average salary of all employees is $125. The average salary of 10 managers is $300 and average salary of workers is $100. What is the total number of employees?

    a. 30
    b. 40
    c. 25
    d. 50

9. In a 30 minute test there are 40 problems. A student solved 28 problems in first 25 minutes. How many seconds should she give to each of the remaining problems?

    a. 20 seconds
    b. 23 seconds
    c. 25 seconds
    d. 27 seconds

10. The total expense of building a fence around a square shaped field is $2000 at a rate of $5 per meter. What is the length of one side?

    a. 80 meters
    b. 100 meters
    c. 40 meters
    d. 320 meters

11. In a class of 83 students, 72 are present. What percent of student is absent? Provide answer up to two significant digits.

    a. 12
    b. 13
    c. 14
    d. 15

12. The price of a product was increased by 45%. If the initial cost of the product was $220, what is the new cost of the product?

    a. $230
    b. $300
    c. $290
    d. $245

13. A worker's weekly salary was increased by 30%. If his new salary is $150, what was his old salary?

   a. $120.00
   b. $99.15
   c. $109.00
   d. $115.40

14. Brad has agreed to buy everyone a Coke. Each drink costs $1.89, and there are 5 friends. Estimate Brad's cost.

   a. $7
   b. $8
   c. $10
   d. $12

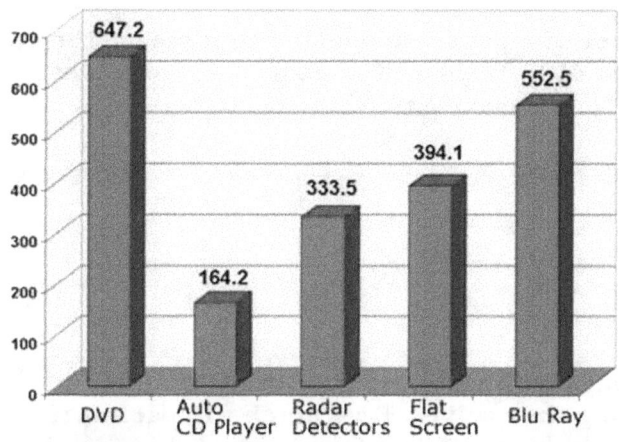

15. Consider the graph above. What is the third best-selling product?

   a. Radar Detectors
   b. Flat Screen TV
   c. Blu Ray
   d. Auto CD Players

16. Which two products are the closest in the number of sales?

    a. Blu Ray and Flat Screen TV
    b. Flat Screen TV and Radar Detectors
    c. Radar Detectors and Auto CD Players
    d. DVD players and Blu Ray

17. Great Britain has a Value Added Tax of 15%. A shop sells a camera for $545. If the VAT is included in the price, what is the actual cost of the camera?

    a. $490.40
    b. $473.91
    c. $505.00
    d. $503.15

18. The owner of a pet store decided to increase the cost of all reptiles 45%. If the initial cost of a reptile was $200, what is the new cost?

    a. $230
    b. $300
    c. $290
    d. $245

19. 5 men have to share a load weighing 10kg 550g equally among themselves. How much will each man have to carry?

    a. 900 g
    b. 1.5 kg
    c. 3 kg
    d. 2 kg 110 g

20. Peter drives 4 blocks to school and back every day. How many blocks does he drive in 5 days?

   a. 20
   b. 30
   c. 40
   d. 50

Part V - Logic

1. Consider the following sequence: 3, 5, 10, 12, 24, ... What 2 numbers should come next?

   a. 48, 58
   b. 26, 28
   c. 48, 50
   d. 26, 52

2. Consider the following sequence: 1000, 992, 984, 976, ... What 2 numbers should come next?

   a. 968, 961
   b. 967, 960
   c. 968, 960
   d. 970, 964

3. Consider the following sequence: 0.1, 0.3, 0.9, 2.7, ... What 2 numbers should come next?

   a. -8.1, -24.3
   b. 8.1, 24.3
   c. 5.4, 10.8
   d. -5.4, -10.8

4. Consider the following sequence: 32, 16, 8, 4, ... What 3 numbers should come next?

    a. 2, 1, 0.5
    b. 2, 0,-2
    c. 0,-4,-8
    d. 2, 1, 0

5. Jane spends her free time reading. She likes to read books, magazines, and even newspapers. She reads stories about adventures and fairy tales.

    a. Jane likes to watch television.
    b. Jane spends her free time writing stories.
    c. Jane's hobby is reading.
    d. Jane reads stories in school.

6. The body is made up of many bones. The skull protects the head. The ribs protect the chest. There are also small bones that protect the ears.

    a. Bones are connected to the muscles.
    b. Bones are present in the stomach.
    c. Animals have bones.
    d. Bones protect different parts of the body.

7. Trees give off oxygen. They also provide shade during sunny days. Some trees bear fruits while others are used to build houses.

    a. Trees have many purposes.
    b. Trees aren't important to men.
    c. Birds build nests in trees.
    d. Roots and trunk are parts of a tree.

8. At a liquor store, five cases of beer are stacked. There are five different types, including, Coors, Budweiser, Heineken, Molsons and Carling Lager.

    1. The Coors is higher than the Carling Lager.

    2. There are two cases between the Carling Lager and Heineken cases.

    3. The Budweiser case is third from the top.

If the bottom case is Carling Lager, which case is on top?

    a. Molsons

    b. Coors

    c. Heineken

    d. Either Molsons or Coors

Instructions for questions 9 and 10.

1. each letter always represents the same word.
2. each word is represented by one letter.
3. the letters are not necessarily in the same order as the words.

    M O R T W means

    Peter loves to text Brittany

    M N X T R means

    Susan loves to text Mark

    Q M X R T means

    Andrea loves to text Susan

    M Z R O Y means

    Gabriel want to email Peter.

9. What letter is "Andrea?"

   a. R
   b. M
   c. Q
   d. Cannot be determined

10. What word is "Z?"

   a. Text
   b. Susan
   c. Gabriel
   d. Cannot be determined.

Scenario: You attend a break and enter and see the suspect leaving the house on Granite St., and runs north. He then turns right on San Pedro, and left on Birch. He cuts through a property on Birch and exits on Richmond. You see him taking the shortcut and continue on San Pedro, turn left on Richmond, and apprehend the suspect on Richmond as he exits the property.

11. What direction was the suspect traveling on San Pedro?

   a. North
   b. South
   c. East
   d. West

12. What direction was the suspect traveling on Birch?

   a. North
   b. South
   c. East
   d. West

13. When you turned left on Richmond, what direction were you traveling?

    a. North

    b. South

    c. East

    d. West

14. Put the statements below into the most logical sequence.

1. A woman calls the station complaining about harassment by her ex husband.
2. You receive the call from dispatch.
3. An officer takes the woman's statement.
4. You question the ex husband.
5. A judge issues a restraining order prohibiting the ex husband from contacting the woman.

    a. 1, 2, 3, 4, 5

    b. 1, 3, 2, 4, 5

    c. 2, 3, 5, 1, 4

    d. 2, 1, 3, 5, 4

15. Put the statements below into the most logical sequence.

1. You ticket one driver for dangerous driving
2. You interview both drivers separately.
3. 2 vehicles collide in the middle of an intersection
4. A vehicles runs a red light.
5. You interview pedestrians on the scene

    a. 1, 2, 3, 4, 5

    b. 1, 3, 2, 4, 5

    c. 2, 3, 5, 1, 4

    d. 4, 3, 2, 5, 1

Answer Key

Reading Comprehension

1. C
Choice C is correct; historians believe it was brutal and bloody. Choice A is incorrect; there is no consensus that the Crusades achieved great things. Choice B is incorrect; it did not stabilize the Holy Lands. Choice D is incorrect, some historians do believe this was the purpose but not all historians.

2. D
The feudal system led to infighting. Choice A is incorrect, it had the opposite effect. Choice B is incorrect, though this is a good answer, it is not the best answer. The Church asked for volunteers not the Feudal Lords. Choice C is incorrect, it did have an effect on the Crusades.

3. A
Saracen was a generic term for Muslims widely used in Europe during the later medieval era.

4. B
This warranty does not cover a product that you have tried to fix yourself. From paragraph two, "This limited warranty does not cover ... any unauthorized disassembly, repair, or modification. "

5. C
ABC Electric could either replace or repair the fan, provided the other conditions are met. ABC Electric has the option to repair or replace.

6. B
The warranty does not cover a stove damaged in a flood. From the passage, "This limited warranty does not cover any damage to the product from improper installation, accident, abuse, misuse, natural disaster, insufficient or excessive electrical supply, abnormal mechanical or environmental

conditions."

A flood is an "abnormal environmental condition," and a natural disaster, so it is not covered.

7. A
A missing part is an example of defective workmanship. This is an error made in the manufacturing process. A defective part is not considered workmanship.

8. D
This question tests the reader's summarization skills. The other choices A, B, and C focus on portions of the second paragraph that are too narrow and do not relate to the specific portion of text in question. The complexity of the sentence may mislead students into selecting one of these answers, but rearranging or restating the sentence will lead the reader to the correct answer. In addition, choice A makes an assumption that may or may not be true about the intentions of the company, choice B focuses on one product rather than the idea of the products, and choice C makes an assumption about women that may or may not be true and is not supported by the text.

9. B
This question tests reader's attention to detail. If a reader selects A, he or she may have picked up on the use of the word "debate" and assumed, very logically, that the two are at odds because they are fighting; however, this is simply not supported in the text. Choice C also uses very specific quotes from the text, but it rearranges and gives them false meaning. The artists want to elevate their creations above the creations of other artists, thereby showing that they are "creative" and "innovative." Similarly, choice D takes phrases straight from the text and rearranges and confuses them. The artists are described as wanting to be "creative, innovative, individual people," not the women.

10. A
This question tests reader's vocabulary and summarization skills. This phrase, used by the author, may seem flippant and dismissive if readers focus on the word "whatever" and misinterpret it as a popular, colloquial term. In this way, choices B and C may mislead the reader to selecting one of

them by including the terms "unimportant" and "stupid," respectively. Choice D is a similar misreading, but doesn't make sense when the phrase is at the beginning of the passage and the entire passage is on media messages. Choice A is literally and contextually appropriate, and the reader can understand that the author would like to keep the introduction focused on the topic the passage is going to discuss.

11. A
This question tests a reader's inference skills. The extreme use of the word "all" in choice B suggests that every single advertising company are working to be approachable, and while this is not only unlikely, the text specifically states that "more" companies have done this, signifying that they have not all participated, even if it's a possibility that they may some day. The use of the limiting word "only" in choice C lends that answer similar problems; women are still buying from companies who do not care about this message, or those companies would not be in business, and the passage specifies that "many" women are worried about media messages, but not all. Readers may find choice D logical, especially if they are looking to make an inference, and while this may be a possibility, the passage does not suggest or discuss this happening. Choice A is correct based on specifically because of the relation between "still working" in the answer and "will hopefully" and the extensive discussion on companies struggles, which come only with progress, in the text.

12. C
This question tests the reader's summarization skills. The entire passage is leading up to the idea that the president of the US may not have had grounds to assert his Fourteen Points when other countries had lost so much. Choice A is pretty directly inferred by the text, but it does not adequately summarize what the entire passage is trying to communicate. Choice B may also be inferred by the passage when it says that the war is "imminent," but it does not represent the entire message, either. The passage does seem to be in praise of FDR, or at least in respect of him, but it does not in any way claim that he is the smartest president, nor does this represent the many other points included. Choice C is then the obvious answer, and most directly relates to the closing sentences which it rewords.

13. C
This question tests the reader's attention to detail. The passage does state that choices A and B are true, and while those statements are in proximity to the explanation for why the war started, they are not the reason given. Choice D is a mix up of words used in the passage, which says that the largest powers were in play but not that this fact somehow started the war. The passage does make a direct statement that a domino effect started the war, supporting choice C as the correct answer.

14. A
This question tests the reader's understanding of functions in writing. Throughout the passage, it states that leaders of other nations were hesitant to accept generous or peaceful terms because of the grievances of the war, and the great loss of life was chief among these. While the passage does touch on the devastation of deadly weapons (B), the use of this raw, emotional fact serves a much larger purpose, and the focus of the passage is not the weapons. While readers may indeed consider who lost the most soldiers (C) when, so many countries were involved and the inequalities of loss are mentioned in the passage, there is no discussion of this in the passage. Choice D is related to A, but choice A is more direct and relates more to the passage.

15. B
This question tests the reader's vocabulary skills. Choice A may seem appealing to readers because it is phonetically similar to "catalyzed," but the two are not related in any other way. Choice C makes sense in context, but if plugged in to the sentence creates a redundancy that doesn't make sense. Choice D does also not make sense contextually, even if the reader may consider that funds were needed to create more weaponry, especially if it was advanced.

16. A
The correct order of ingredients is brown sugar, baking soda and chocolate chips.

17. B
Sturdy: strong, solid in structure or person. In context, Stir in chocolate chips by hand with a *sturdy* wooden spoon.

18. A
Disperse: to scatter in different directions or break up. In context, Stir until the chocolate chips and nuts are evenly *dispersed.*

19. B
You can stop stirring the nuts when they are evenly distributed. From the passage, "Stir until the chocolate chips and nuts are evenly dispersed."

20. B
Choice A is incorrect as the Monster killed Frankenstein, not the other way around. Choice B is correct, Frankenstein is dead. Choice C is incorrect - Mary Shelley is the author. Choice D is incorrect, the person is called Frankenstein.

Part II - Judgment, Recognition and Observation

Section I - Professional Judgment

1. C
One of your responsibilities is the safety, which includes yourself. In addition, a high speed chase could endanger innocent people. The best course of action is to follow the cars at a high but safe speed and update dispatch with a description of the cars and any other information you have.

2. B
A primary responsibility is to your fellow officers and this is much more important than your meeting.

3. A
The best course of action is the gather more information and then proceed from there.

4.B
Protection of life is a primary responsibility of a police officer

so the best course of action is to investigate the complaint immediately. You can finish lunch later.

5. C
Handling the situation carefully and calmly is important. Stay calm and do not engage. Explain that you have found him apparently leaving the scene of a crime and would like to ask some questions

6. A
While it is important to handle the situation carefully, you have already warned him once and explained the situation. Staying calm, the best course of action is to explain that if he continues to refuse, you will have to take him to the station for questioning

7. B
The best course of action is to ask if everything is OK. No crime is being committed, and no one is being injured.

Section II - Recognition and Identification

8. A
Choice A is the same person. Choice B, while having different hair and wearing sunglasses has a wider face. Choice C and D have narrower faces.

9. A
Choice A is the same person. Choice B has a thinner face. Choice D and D have wider faces.

10. A
Choice A is the same person. Choices B and D have wider faces. Choice C has a narrower face.

Section III - Observation

11. B
Janet Benoit is wanted for child neglect.

12. C
Jeffrey Crisp is wanted for sexual assault.

13. C
The Volkswagen Phaeton is from Ontario.

14. D
Nathan Abraham is wanted for domestic assault.

15. A
The modified Chevrolet truck is from the Yukon.

Part III - Composition

1. A
Anecdote: n. A short account of an incident

2. B
Heinous: adj. shocking, terrible or wicked.

3. A
Harbinger: n. a person of thing that tells or announces the coming of someone or something

4. B
Judicious: Having, or characterized by, good judgment or sound thinking. Careful.

5. B
Ethanol: n. a colorless volatile flammable liquid C_2H_6O.

6. A
Respiratory: adj. Of, relating to, or affecting respiration or the organs of respiration.

7. B
Inherent: Naturally a part or consequence of something.

8. A
Vapid: adj. tasteless or bland.

9. C
Waif: n. homeless child or stray.

10. D
Homologous: adj. similar or identical.

11. A
Correspondence is the correct spelling.

12. C
Hemorrhage is the correct spelling.

13. B
Environment is the correct spelling.

14. D
Government is the correct spelling.

15. C
Conceive is the correct spelling.

16. A
Describe is the correct spelling.

17. B
Liquor is the correct spelling.

18. D
Successful is the correct spelling.

19. B
Hurricane is the correct spelling.

20. A
Precede is the correct spelling.

21. D
A colon informs the reader that what follows the mark proves, explains, or lists elements of what preceded the mark.

22. D
A colon informs the reader that what follows the mark proves, explains, or lists elements of what preceded the mark.

23. C
The dash is used when the speaker cannot continue.

24. D
Healthful vs. Healthy. Use 'Healthy' to describe something that is of good for your health and 'healthful' refers to habits or types.

25. A
In vs. Into. 'In' a room means inside. 'Into' refers to movement or action.

26. C
Lay vs. Lie. 'Lie' requires an object and 'lay' does not. So you can lie down, (no object. and you lay a book on the floor.

27. B
Lose vs. Loose. 'Lose' is to no longer have, or to lose a race. 'Loose' is not tied or able to move freely.

28. D
Persecute vs. Prosecute. To prosecute is to have a legal claim against someone and to persecute is to harass.

29. A
Precede vs. Proceed. To precede, is to go first or in front of. To proceed is to go forward.

30. C
Rise vs. Raise. 'Rise' does not require an object and raise does require an object. You have to 'raise' something.

Part V – Math

1. D
2009 X 108 is about 210,000. The actual number is 216,972.

2. A
The price of 12 shirts with profit is 8% = 0.92 X 336 = $309.12 The purchase price of each shirt = 309.12/12 = $25.76

3. D
Substitute the known variables, (3 x 2) + (4 x 4) x 8 =, 6 + 16 x 8, 24 x 8 = 176

4. A
2cnx = 2(4 x 5 x 3)/(2 X 5) =, 2 x 60/2 x 5 =, 120/10 = 12

5. D
Substitute with known variables, (6 x 8) – 12 + (2 x 12) =, 48 – 12 + 24, do the additions first, 48 – (12 + 24) =, 48 – 36 = 12

6. A
$\sqrt{121}$ = 11

7. D
To find the total turnout in all three polling stations, we need to proportion the number of voters to the number of all registered voters.
Number of total voters = 945 + 860 + 1210 = 3015

Number of total registered voters = 1270 + 1050 + 1440 = 3760

Percentage turnout over all three polling stations = 3015 * 100/3760 = 80.19%

Checking the answers, we round 80.19 to the nearest whole number: 80%

8. B
Assume the total numbers of employees is x. The total salary of all employees will be 125x. The total salary of the managers = 10 X 300 = $3000. The number of employees = X - 10, so the total salary of employees will be 100 X (X-10). The equation becomes 100(X - 10) + 3000 = 125X. x = 40.

9. C
The number of remaining questions is 40 - 28 = 12
The time remaining is 30 - 25 = 5 minutes = 5 X 60 = 300 seconds. So the time remaining for each question is 300/12 = 25 seconds.

10. B
Total expense is $2000 and we are informed that $5 is spent per meter. Combining these two information, we know that the total length of the fence is 2000/5 = 400 meters.

The fence is built around a square shaped field. If one side of the square is "a," the perimeter of the square is "4a." Here, the perimeter is equal to 400 meters. So,

400 = 4a

100 = a → this means that one side of the square is equal to 100 meters.

11. B
If 72 students are present, then 83 - 72 = 11 students are absent. To calculate the percent, the equation will be,

11/83 = x/100
83x = 1100
x = 1100/83
x = 13.25   rounding off - 13% of the students are absent.

12. C
Initial cost was $220. new cost = 200 + 45% of 200, 45% of 200, 45/100 x 200 = 90, therefore new price is 200 + 90 = $290

13. D
Let old salary = X, therefore $150 = x + 0.30x, 150 = 1x + 0.30x, 150 = 1.30x, x = 150/1.30 = 115.4

14. C
If there are 5 friends and each drink costs $1.89, we can round up to $2 per drink and estimate the total cost at, 5 X $2 = $10.

The actual, cost is 5 X $1.89 = $9.45.

15. B
Flat Screen TVs are the third best-selling product.

16. B
The two products that are closest in the number of sales, are Flat Screen TVs and Radar Detectors.

17. B
Actual cost = X, therefore, 545 = x + 0.15x, 545 = 1x + 0.15x, 545 = 1.15x, x = 545/1.15 = 473.91

18. C
Initial cost was $220. new cost = 200 + 45% of 200, 45% of 200, 45/100 x 200 = 90, therefore new price is 200 + 90 = $290

19. D
First convert the unit of measurements to be the same.
Since 1000 g = 1 kg, 10 kg = 10 x 1000 = 10,000 + 550 g = 10,550 g. Divide 10,550 by 5 = 10550/5 = 2110 = 2 kg 110 g

20. C
Each round trip will be 8 blocks, so in 5 days, he will drive 5 X 8 = 40 blocks.

Part V - Logic

1. D
The sequence is increasing by adding 2 and multiplying 2 alternatively. The next 2 terms are 24 + 2= 26 and 26 x 2 = 52.

2. C
The sequence is decreasing by 8.

3. B
The sequence is increasing by multiplying each the last term by 3. 2.7 x 3= 8.1 and 8.1 x 3 = 24.3

4. A
The sequence is decreasing by dividing the last term by 2.

5. C
The only certain thing is Jane's hobby is reading.

6. D
The only certain thing is bones protect different parts of the body.

7. A
The only certain thing is tree have many purposes.

8. C
Given information is that Carling Lager is on the bottom, and #3 says Budweiser is 3rd from the top. #2 says there are two cases between the Carling Lager and Heineken cases, so the Heineken case must be in position 2.

1.
2. Heineken case
3. Budweiser case
4.
5. Carling Lager case

Molsons and Coors are still unknown. #1 says the Coors case is higher than the Carling Lager case, but since we know the Carling Lager case is on the bottom, that doesn't help. Therefore, we cannot determine the positions of the Molsons or Coors cases.

9. C
"Andrea" is only in sentence 3. Since all three sentences only differ in the names, the corresponding letters found in all three, M R and T must be "loves to text."

"Susan" must correspond to "X," as they both appear in sentences 2 and 3. To find "Andrea," which only appears in sentence 3, look for the only other letter in that sentence, which is Q.

10. D
"M" and "R" appear in all four sentences, so they must be "loves" and "to" which also appear in all four.

The letters "Z" and "Y" only appear in sentence #4. The other difference between sentence #4 are the words "email" and "Gabriel," but we cannot determine which.

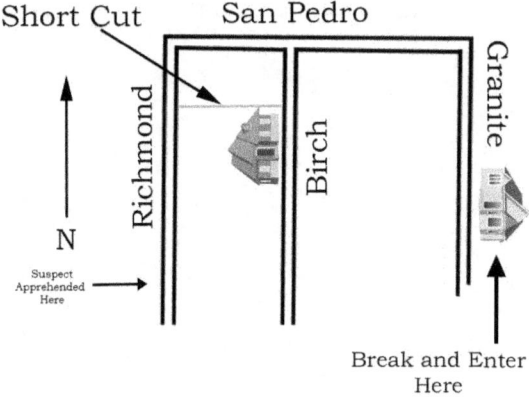

11. D
The suspect was travelling west on San Pedro.

12. B
The suspect was travelling south on Birch.

13. B
You were travelling south when you turned left on Richmond.

14. B
1, 3, 2, 4, 5 is the correct sequence.

1. A woman calls the station complaining about harassment by her ex husband.
3. An officer takes the woman's statement.
2. You receive the call from dispatch.
4. You question the ex husband.
5. A judge issues a restraining order prohibiting the ex husband from contacting the woman.

15. D
4, 3, 2, 5, 1 is the correct sequence.

4. A vehicles runs a red light.
3. 2 vehicles collide in the middle of an intersection
2. You interview both drivers separately.
5. You interview pedestrians on the scene
1. You ticket one driver for dangerous driving

Conclusion

Congratulations! You have made it this far because you have applied yourself diligently to practicing for the exam and no doubt improved your potential score considerably! Getting into a good school is a huge step in a journey that might be challenging at times but will be many times more rewarding and fulfilling. That is why being prepared is so important.

Good Luck!

Free Ebook Version

http://tinyurl.com/jm23rh9

www.ingramcontent.com/pod-product-compliance
Lightning Source LLC
LaVergne TN
LVHW010301260326
834688LV00044B/1399